ENGLISH ❖ HERITAGE

Book of
Roman London

… despite the rubble and the rain,
Great wonders come to light again.

Kate Milne, 1981

ENGLISH✛HERITAGE

Book of
Roman
London

Urban archaeology in the nation's capital

Gustav Milne

B.T. Batsford / English Heritage

963.
2104
Mil

© Gustav Milne 1995

First published 1995

Typeset by DP Press Ltd, Sevenoaks

Printed and bound in Great Britain by
The Bath Press, Bath

Published by B.T. Batsford Ltd
4 Fitzhardinge Street, London W1H 0AH

A CIP catalogue record for this book is
available from the British Library

ISBN 0 7134 6851 3 (cased)
0 7134 6852 1 (limp)

Contents

List of illustrations ... 7

List of colour plates ... 9

Acknowledgements ... 10

Preface ... 11

1 Historical sources: a meagre haul ... 15

2 Rescuing Londinium ... 20

3 Dating the data ... 32

4 An undistinguished settlement? ... 39

5 New town ... 48

6 Capital city ... 56

7 From Londinium to Augusta ... 71

8 Answers and questions ... 90

9 Rebuilding Londinium ... 97

10 All creatures great and small (*with Barbara West*) ... 106

11 Citizens (*with Francis Grew*) ... 113

12 The remains of Roman London ... 120

Further reading ... 123

Glossary ... 125

Index ... 126

Illustrations

1 City of London, with position of main Roman features shown 12
2 London and the Antonine Itinerary 17
3 Investigating the Regis House site in 1930 21
4 Recording the Temple of Mithras, 1954 22
5 Excavations at St Swithin's House 1950 23
6 Volunteers in London in the 1960s 24
7 Archaeologists working on the Roman waterfront in 1981 25
8 First-century quay at Pudding Lane 25
9 Basement excavations in 1981 27
10 Watching brief: archaeologists vs. machines 28
11 Planning in the Roman basilica, 1985 29
12 Finds store 30
13 Roman coin *in situ* from the Leadenhall Court site 33
14 Roman pottery 34
15 Computers and archaeology in 1983 35
16 Third-century Samian pottery from the New Fresh Wharf site 36
17 Third-century timber-faced quay 37
18 Plan of London showing the natural topography 40
19 Plan of London showing main roads in relation to the natural topography 41
20 Plan of London showing extent of settlement in AD 55 43
21 First-century round house from the Newgate Street site 44
22 Plan of mid-first-century buildings on the Newgate Street site 45

23 Mid-first-century buildings on the Bucklersbury site 47
24 Plan of developments on the Leadenhall Court site 49
25 First-century buildings on the Leadenhall Court site 50
26 Town houses in the late first century from the Leadenhall Court site 51
27 Plan of town centre laid out in the late first century 52
28 Recording the Roman forum in the Gracechurch Street tunnel 53
29 Huggin Hill bath-house in 1969 54
30 Plan of London showing extent of settlement in AD 80 55
31 Plans showing development of civic centre, from AD 85 to 140 57
32 Part of the masonry and brick-built walls of the second-century basilica 58
33 Plan of London showing extent of settlement in early second century 59
34 Recording the Huggin Hill bath-house in 1989 59
35 The eastern entrance to the amphitheatre at Guildhall Yard 60
36 Plan showing the amphitheatre in relation to medieval Guildhall 61
37 Well-preserved timber baseplate from a building in the Walbrook valley 62
38 Excavating a brickearth walled building in the upper Walbrook valley 62
39 Roman hobnailed boots from London 63
40 Plan of leather and glass-working buildings in the Walbrook valley 63

41 Plan of the second-century harbour 64
42 Recording a timber-floored waterfront warehouse 65
43 Roman quayside recorded at Pudding Lane 66
44 Town houses in the second century 67
45 Residential building on the Watling Court site 68
46 Tessellated pavement from building on the Whittington Avenue site 69
47 Lifting the mosaic pavement from the Milk Street site 70
48 Excavating dark grey silts overlying the Roman horizon at Newgate Street 71
49 Mosaic pavement on the Bank of England site, 1934 73
50 Plan of late Roman town houses at Austin Friars 74
51 Third-century arcaded building on the Queen Street site 75
52 Monumental Arch from Baynard's Castle 76
53 Monumental foundations laid in AD 294 at St Peter's Hill 77
54 Section through the defences of Londinium 77
55 Roman city wall exposed at Crosswall 77
56 Waterfront development in Roman London 80
57 Third-century harbourworks on the Thames Exchange site 82
58 Roman road in the early second century 83
59 Roman road in the fourth century 83

60 Recording the riverside wall at Baynard's Castle 84
61 Foundations of a projecting bastion at Crosswall 85
62 Late Roman buildings 86
63 Late fourth-century building at Pudding Lane 87
64 Plan of London showing line of late Roman defensive wall 88
65 Changing interpretations of the London basilica 91
66 Changing interpretations of the 'Governor's Palace' 92
67 Londinium and Britannia 95
68 Reconstruction of a Roman timber-framed building 98
69 Reconstruction of the basilica 100
70 Reconstruction of the timber bridge 102
71 Building a Roman boat 104
72 Wet sieving soil samples to recover fish and bird bones 106
73 Barn owl in the basilica 107
74 Dog burial below house foundation on the Newgate Street site 110
75 Excavating a Roman Londoner 111
76 Cemetery excavations at Giltspur Street, 1989 112
77 Third-century altar from Baynard's Castle 114
78 Marble inscription from Winchester Palace 116
79 Tombstone from Crosswall 119
80 Plan of London showing surviving Roman features 121

Colour Plates

(Between pages 64 and 65)

1 Londinium AD 60
2 Second-century building from Newgate Street
3 Londinium in the second century
4 Statue of Mercury
5 Second-century harbour
6 Roman waterfront excavations in 1981

7 Bakehouse in Londinium
8 Painted wall plaster figure
9 Basilica excavations in 1985
10 Imported pottery
11 Building in Londinium in AD 293
12 Dark grey silts over the mosaic pavement at Milk Street

Acknowledgements

A book of this type must obviously encapsulate the research of many people, only some of whom are acknowledged in the all too brief bibliography (see pp 123–4); it was not possible to insert references in the text to show precisely where all the ideas came from. My first debt must be to all those who worked for and with the Department of Urban Archaeology, as volunteers or professionals, upon whose labours this book was built. There is not space to name them all, but I hope those whose contribution remains anonymous are not offended. For the bulk of the book, I admit to having drawn heavily on the work of the late, much-lamented Ralph Merrifield, and of W. F. Grimes, Peter Marsden and Dominic Perring, as well as of Nicholas Bateman, Trevor Brigham, David Bentley, Damian Goodburn, Francis Grew, Catherine Maloney, John Maloney, Michael Rhodes, Steven Roskams, Peter Rowsome, John Shepherd, Ian Tyers, Paul Tyers, Tim Williams and Tony Wilmott, and upon reports or discussions with Ian Betts, Ian Blair, Gary Brown, Mark Burch, Carrie Cowan, Naomi Crowley, Anne Davis, Jo Groves, Friedrike Hammer, Charles Hill, Julian Hill, Duncan Lees, Dominique de Moulins, Bill McCann, Frances Pritchard, Dave Sankey, Harvey Sheldon, Angela Wardle, Robert Whytehead, Paul Wootton and Brian Yule, as well as Richard McPhail and Professor Richard Battarbee (both of University College London) and Tom Blagg (University of Kent).

For Chapter 3, the work of Barbara Davies, Jenny Hall, Ian Tyers and Jennifer Hillam (University of Sheffield) is gratefully acknowledged. Chapter 10 benefits from the work of Phillip Armitage, Annie Grant, Derreck Rixson, Tony King, Jessica Winder, Alison Locker and Tony Waldron, but most especially from Barbara West. Particular mention must be made of Francis Grew (Museum of London) who made many helpful comments on an early draft of the text, and contributed considerably to Chapter 11. Nevertheless, I alone am responsible for inaccuracies and misinterpretations of the research embodied in this study.

The photograph on fig. 73 is reproduced by kind permission of Robert T. Smith, while the other photographs were printed by Andy Chopping and Maggie Cox of the Museum of London Archaeology Service, and are reproduced with the permission of the Museum of London. The other illustrations were expertly produced by a variety of hands, including Sue Hurman (figs 39, 52, 54, 77–9); Susan Banks (fig. 69); Martin Bentley (colour plate 7); Peter Froste (colour plate 11); Damian Goodburn (fig. 68) and John Pearson (colour plates 1, 3). However, the majority of the artwork was by Chrissie Milne, who laboured long and hard and also contributed to the book in many other ways. Finally, to Charlotte Kilenyi, Peter Kemmis Betty and Stephen Johnson for their faith, hope and charity.

Preface

The City of London's first fulltime archaeological unit began work on the cold but optimistic morning of 3 December 1973. The Department of Urban Archaeology (DUA) was inauspiciously inaugurated in the foyer of the Guildhall Museum, when four diggers were given instructions by Peter Marsden who, until that day, had been the sole official responsible for the City's archaeology. We made our way to a site in the Cripplegate Fort (discovered by Professor Grimes in the late 1940s) to cut and record two sections, a job that would take us about a week. By then, the new Unit Director would have arrived with new instructions for the new era. Thus the first official DUA excavation got underway on an overgrown site, using barrows and spades borrowed from the Corporation of London works department. It was fitting that our first project should have been to extend the work of Professor Grimes, and that the key to the Noble Street site should have been handed over to us by Peter Marsden, for the successes which the DUA can claim were firmly founded on the work of those two pioneers. This book is an assessment of Roman London based on what happened next: nearly two decades of unprecedented rescue excavations and research by what became the largest urban archaeological unit in Europe.

Preservation by record

Throughout the 18-year period of the DUA's operations, most of the post-excavation analysis and a significant proportion of the fieldwork, notably in the 1970s, was funded by the Department of the Environment through the Inspectorate of Ancient Monuments, the body now known as English Heritage. The brief of that organisation is to preserve the national heritage: however, the preservation of Roman remains *in situ* was an expensive option in the 1970s and '80s if it involved re-designing the foundations of a new building. In such cases, 'preservation by record' was preferred, whereby the remains were destroyed to make way for the new structure, but not before an 'adequate' archaeological record of the site had been compiled. As a direct consequence of that policy, although little of Roman London survives as a visible monument today, we now have a vast collection of records, measured drawings, photographs and artefacts from which a detailed history of the settlement can be reconstructed. This book is therefore offered in part as a justification of the 'preservation by record' maxim: although most of the physical evidence of Londinium has now been destroyed, at least one can read about it.

But the digging of a site is only the start of the study, representing just the collection of raw data, no more and no less. Our understanding of the past comes through careful assessment of those raw data, refined, phased, dated, compared and contrasted. Only after a site has been researched and published has it really been 'saved': preservation by field record is not enough, preservation by publication is what is needed. This point needs stressing for the simple reason that 70% of the DUA's excavations are as yet unpublished. Developers are often reluctant to fund the less visible parts of the programme, and so the burden falls almost entirely upon English Heritage, who have provided strong support for City archaeology for this specific purpose, particularly from 1984 to 1991. During that period, they funded a programme which attempted to bring to publication the first ten years-worth of DUA excavations, which included over 70 Roman sites. This book summarises some of that work, while attempting to show how great the potential for further study still is: over the last decade, the pace of excavation has so completely outstripped that of publication that the Museum of London now has a larger backlog of unpublished material in 1993 than it had in 1973.

The first chapters in this book present the background to the study, opening with a summary of the scanty 'historical' records of the Roman town (Chapter 1): the sometimes acrimonious tale of how the search for London's past was organised (Chapter 2), together with discussions of the dating methodologies now used to such dramatic effect follow (Chapter 3).

In Chapters 4–7, evidence for the development of Londinium is presented, highlighting some of the more significant aspects of a notably changing townscape between AD 50 and AD 450: parts of that picture are then evaluated in Chapter 8. The material included in a work of this length is necessarily highly selective, providing an (I stress *an*, not *the*) interpretation of *archaeological* evidence for the town's history. An attempt is made to identify principal trends in

1 *Modern street plan of the City of London, with the position of some features of Roman Londinium superimposed upon it, including the line of the town wall, the fort at Cripplegate, the amphitheatre, the forum and the bridge (Chrissie Milne).*

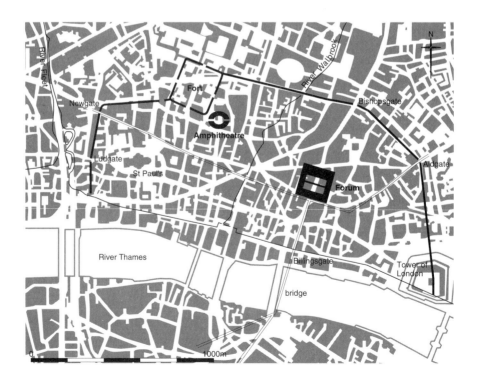

the development process, drawing in particular upon the larger excavation projects and the more recent research. The principal focus of this study is the settlement contained within the line of City wall on the north bank of the Thames between Blackfriars Bridge, the Barbican, Bishopsgate and the Tower, since this is the area in which the DUA operated (**1**). However, reference is necessarily made to activity on the equally important Roman developments on the south bank at Southwark from records collected by our sister unit, the Department of Greater London Archaeology (DoGLA). In conclusion, exercises in reconstructing the Roman town (Chapter 9), a study of animal bones (Chapter 10) and a survey of the inscriptions from Roman London are appended (Chapter 11).

There have already been several excellent general books written on Londinium (see Chapter 13), but as more evidence becomes available, even more books will be needed to synthesize and interpret the data. The present volume makes no claim to being the final word on such an evolving subject: its main aim is to show something of what the DUA achieved between 1973 and 1991, with regard to the Roman town (the Medieval excavations merit a book of their own). It is a summary of urban rescue archaeology at its most intense, and how it rediscovered Londinium.

Gustav Milne
Institute of Archaeology
University College London

1

Historical sources: a meagre haul

The study of Roman London's past can be approached from different directions: the historian works with whatever written records have survived, the archaeologist studies the physical evidence of the town, two quite separate sets of data, different in quantity and in kind. Initially at least, these two sources should be treated separately, for both need careful assessment and interpretation by their respective specialists: an archaeologist who cannot speak Latin will not understand the subtleties of written references any more than a classicist who has never excavated will be able to interpret a complex archaeological sequence. The archaeologists working in London during the last 20 years have seen a seemingly never-ending body of data build up from site after site, day by day, year on year, as will be seen in the rest of this book.

In stark contrast the surviving documentary record for Londinium, the raw material from which the classical historian must wrest the town's history, presents a meagre haul. The sum total of the evidence from contemporary classical sources is summarised below (together with contributions from some post-Roman writers) in translation, taken principally from the RCHM volume on Roman London published in 1928. It is not strictly correct to say that the Roman historian's haul was finite, since archaeology is also discovering written data, in the form of inscriptions from buildings or tombstones, graffiti, writing tablets, and so forth: this corpus is summarised separately in Chapter 11.

There are therefore but fourteen direct documentary references to the City listed below, and, of these, half are merely incidental mentions on maps, lists or in geographies. Of the remainder, one is of first-century date; there are none at all from the second to mid-third century; one from the late third and four from the fourth century. The corpus seems fixed and finite: there have been no new discoveries of annals, panegyrics or epic poems in Roman London in the last 20 years.

AD 43: Roman Invasion

This passage, by Cassius Dio (*c.* AD 150–235), is thought to describe the London area during the Roman invasion in AD 43, although it was written 100 years later:

> Thence the Britons retired to the River Thames at a point where it empties into the ocean and at flood-tide forms a lake. This they easily crossed because they knew where the firm ground and the easy passages in the region were to be found; but the Romans in attempting to follow them were not so successful. However, the Germans swam across again and some of the others got over by a bridge a little way up-stream, after which they assailed the barbarians from several sides at once and cut down many of them. In pursuing the remainder incautiously, they got into swamps from which it was difficult to make their way out, and so lost a number of men.

AD 61: Boudican uprising

Following the sacking of the new provincial capital at Camulodunum (Colchester), the Britons led by Queen Boudica turned towards the Roman settlements of Londinium and Verulamium (St Albans). This oft-quoted report incorporates the earliest surviving direct reference to Londinium, dated to either AD 60 or 61. The 'businessmen and merchandise' (*negotiatorum et commeatuum*) mentioned below probably refers to military supply contracts, rather than purely civilian trade. It is worth stressing that the author, the historian Cornelius Tacitus (*c.* AD 55–120), was only six at the time of the rebellion and never actually visited Britain. His source was his father-in-law Julius Agricola who was serving in the province as a military tribune at the time of the rebellion, and was a legionary commander there in *c.* AD 70–3 returning as governor in AD 78–84:

> But Suetonius (the Governor), undismayed, marched through disaffected territory to Londinium. This town was not distinguished by the title of 'colonia', but was an important centre for businessmen and merchandise. At first he hesitated whether to stand and fight there. Eventually, his numerical inferiority – and the price only too clearly paid by the rashness of the divisional commander (who had earlier been defeated by the rebels) – decided him to sacrifice the single city of Londinium to save the province as a whole. Unmoved by lamentations and appeals, Suetonius gave the signal for departure. The inhabitants were allowed to accompany him. But those who stayed because they were women, or old, or attached to the place, were slaughtered by the enemy. Verulamium suffered the same fate.

> The natives enjoyed plundering and thought of nothing else. By-passing forts and garrisons, they made for where loot was richest and protection weakest. Roman and provincial deaths at the places mentioned (Londinium, Camulodunum and Verulamium) are estimated at 70,000. For the British did not take or sell prisoners, or practice other war time exchanges. They could not wait to cut throats, hang, burn and crucify – as though avenging, in advance, the retribution that was on its way.

Mid second century: Ptolemy's Geography

Claudius Ptolemeus of Alexandria (*c.* AD 100–51) compiled his *Geography*, a gazetteer of peoples and places, in Greek. It contains three direct references to London:

a) Noviomagus was 59 miles more to the south than Londinium in Britain.

b) Next to the Silures, the most easterly are the Cantii, amongst whom the principal cities are Londinium and Rutupiae.

c) In the island of Albion, Londinium has its greatest day of 18 hours.

AD 193–208

Although there is no direct reference to London by name in the events of this period, it is known that the British governor Clodius Albinus mounted an unsuccessful rebellion which ended in his defeat at the hands of his rival, Septimius Severus. The province was invaded by the Roman army once more, and was subsequently divided into two, Londinium becoming the capital of *Britannia Superior*.

Early third century: Antonine itinerary

A record of fifteen main roads in the province (2) shows that route no. II from Rutupiae (Richborough), a principal port on the south coast, to Hadrian's Wall in the extreme north, passes through London. Seven other routes begin or end at London:

no. III to Dubris (Dover);
no. IV to Portus Lemanis (Lympne);
no. V to Luguvalio ad Vallum (Carlisle) via Eburacum (York);
no. VI to Lindum (Lincoln);
no. VII to Regno (Chichester);
no. VIII to Eburacum (York);
no. IX to Venta Icinorum (Caistor by Norwich) via Camulodunum (Colchester).

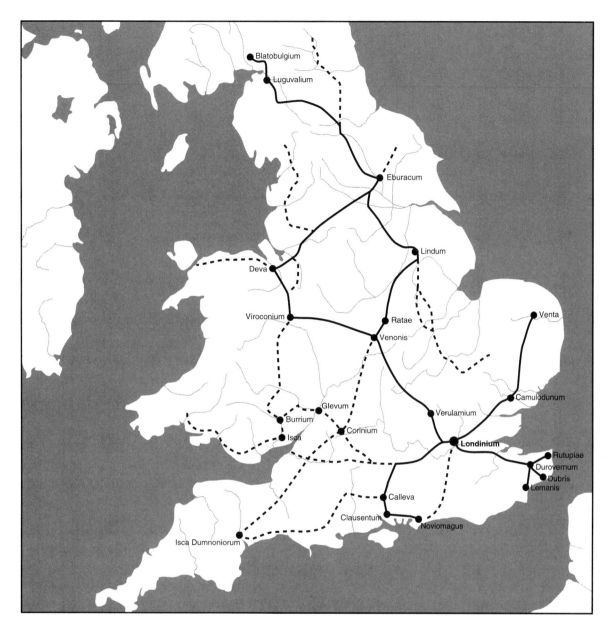

AD 296: rebellion of Allectus

In AD 286, the British governor Carausius illegally declared himself emperor of Britain. He was subsequently murdered and succeeded in AD 293 by his one-time colleague, the ambitious Allectus. In AD 296 Britain was invaded by another Roman army, this time led by Constantius Chlorus in a successful attempt to win back the province from the usurper Allectus. This event is commemorated by the famous

2 *London and the Antonine Itinerary. Routes passing through Londinium (London) are shown black; other main roads are shown dashed* (Chrissie Milne).

Arras medallion, which shows Londinium (*Lon*) welcoming Constantius Chlorus (the restorer of eternal light). In the aftermath of this rebellion, the province was divided into four, of which Londinium was presumed to be the capital of *Maxima Caesariensis*. This record of the events is

17

from the Panegyric to Constantius composed by Eumenius (AD 260–311):

> Unconquered Caesar … those of your troops who … reached London found the survivors of the barbarian mercen-aries plundering the city and, when these began to seek flight, landed and slew them in the streets. And not only did they bring safety to your subjects by the timely destruction of the enemy, but, also induced a sentiment of gratitude and pleasure at the sight.

AD 314: Council of Arles

Following Constantine's conversion to Christianity in 312, many clerics were invited to attend a council at Arles including:

> … Eborius, bishop of York in the province of Britain, Restitutus, bishop of London in the said province; Adelfius, bishop of ?Lincoln.

AD 360: invasion of Picts and Scots

The fourth century saw the province increasingly under threat from barbarian incursions. The next three passages are from the *Rerum Gestarum*, by Ammianus Marcellinus (*c.* 325–90).

> … the general [Lupicinius] came in the midst of winter to Boulogne; and collecting transports and embarking his troops, he sailed with a fair wind to Richborough on the opposite coast. Thence he marched to London, that he might take such decision as the aspect of affairs demanded and might more quickly hasten to take the task in hand

AD 367–8: barbarian conspiracy

The province was overrun by a concerted wave of invasions by Picts, Scots and Saxons, and was only restored after a full scale invasion by a Roman army led by Count Theodosius. The accounts of these events are the first record that Londinium had recently been renamed *Augusta*.

> (Theodosius) … reached Boulogne … he crossed the strait in a leisurely manner and reached Richborough, a sheltered haven on the opposite coast. And when the Batavi and Heruli and the Jovian and Victorian legions

> … had also arrived, he then, relying on the force of numbers, landed and marched towards London, an ancient town which has since been named Augusta; … he attacked the predatory and straggling bands of the enemy who were loaded with the weight of their plunder, and having speedily routed them while driving prisoners in chains and cattle before them, he deprived them of their booty which they had carried off from these miserable tributaries of Rome … Amid scenes of jubilation which recalled a Roman triumph, he made his entry into the city which had just before been overwhelmed by disasters, but was now suddenly re-established almost before it could have hoped for deliverance.

AD 369: Britannia recovered

> Theodosius … marched with resolution from Augusta, which the ancients used to call Londinium, with an army which he had collected with great energy and skill; bringing a mighty aid to the embarrassed and disturbed fortunes of the Britons. … He vanquished the various tribes in whom their past security had engendered an insolence which led them to attack the Roman territories: and he entirely restored the cities and the fortresses which through the manifold disasters of the time had been injured or destroyed, though they had been founded to secure the age-long tranquillity of the country.

c. AD 400: *Notitia Dignitatum*

The *Notitia* is a late Roman collection of administrative information, including lists of civil officials as well as the disposition of various military units and personnel. The report records that there was '… an Officer in charge of the Treasury at Augusta [London]'.

c. AD 457: Anglo-Saxon Chronicle

The Roman legions serving in Britannia were withdrawn for service elsewhere in the beleaguered empire, and were not replaced: by *c.* AD 410 the province had to look to its own defence against invaders whom later writers called Angles, Saxons and Jutes. The Chronicle was compiled from the late ninth century onwards, and was written, not in Latin, but in the contemporary English language:

> In this year Hengest and Aesc fought against the Britons at a place called Crecganford [Crayford, Kent] and there slew four companies; and the Britons then forsook Kent and fled to London in great terror.

Early sixth century: Stephen of Byzantium

Stephen compiled a geographical dictionary which included this reference: 'Lindonion, a city of Britain; … the name of the inhabitants is Lindonini.'

AD 604: Bede's Ecclesiastical History of the English Nation

The province was ultimately overrun by the pagan Saxon peoples, who were subsequently converted to Christianity. The Venerable Bede (673–735) probably never visited London himself, but wrote his famous *History* in Latin in a Northumbrian monastery, over 100 years after the event recorded here:

> Augustine, archbishop of Britain, ordained two bishops, viz Mellitus and Justus: Mellitus to preach to the province of the East Saxons [Essex] who are divided from Kent by the river Thames and border on the Eastern Sea. Their metropolis is the city of London, which is situated on the banks of the aforesaid river, and is the mart of many nations resorting to it be sea and land.

Early seventh century: the Martyrology of St Jerome

An obscure document apparently compiled from fifth-century sources mentions the otherwise unknown fourth-century bishop Augulus, '… born in the town of Augusta in Britannia.'

Seventh century: the Ravenna Cosmography

This document contains a list of over 5000 place names from the Roman world, compiled from various sources by a clerk in Ravenna, a seat of government in the Byzantine empire until AD 751. It mentions London three times as: 'Londinis, Landini' and 'Londinium Augusti'.

A history of Londinium

Taken as a whole, these references are neither as detailed nor as evenly distributed over time as one would like, although they do at least provide the name of our settlement. Working solely from written data it can be suggested that Londinium was founded before AD 60, that it was not initially ranked as a *municipium* (i.e., a chartered town), that a proportion of its population was engaged in trade, that it had no major defences and, as a consequence, suffered horribly in the uprising of AD 61. The fact that old people and women are mentioned as living there implies that the settlement had been in existence for some time, and must have been of some consequence, even if of uncertain legal status, to be discussed alongside the *municipium* of Verulamium and the capital of Camulodunum. The figure quoted for the number of dead in the three settlements means little more than 'a substantial number', and provides no guide to the population of any of the towns at this time. Although the precious fragment from Tacitus provides us with a remarkable opening view of Londinium, those few lines represent the most detailed account of the Roman city to have survived. Its position and extent are not recorded, neither are there any topographical details regarding street plan, buildings, or public facilities.

The other records suggest that the town lay at a crucial junction of the road network, was prosperous enough to be worth sacking, and was also known by the name of *Augusta* by the mid fourth century. It was sufficiently important to have a bishop and house the treasury and seems, at first glance, to have maintained its existence in spite of the Saxon invasions into the seventh century. Later chapters show to what extent the archaeological evidence collected over a twenty-year period confirms, complements or contradicts such inferences.

2

Rescuing Londinium

1800–1973: against all odds

The story of how our understanding of Roman London has been achieved is almost as dramatic as the chequered history of the settlement itself. It is not a tale of steady progress, in which each new generation builds purposefully and expansively upon the work of their predecessors, but rather a series of disconnected peaks of real achievement separated by considerable troughs of Philistine disregard on the part of authorities or developers. For archaeological research to prosper in the shadow of relentless urban development, the archaeologists need the active support and co-operation of the developers who wish to build, the Corporation of London who are responsible for local planning matters, central government which is concerned with ancient monument legislation, the local museum which should set the research agenda and keep a secure archive and, last but not least, the general public, whose heritage is threatened by unsympathetic redevelopment. It has rarely proved possible to keep all five of these diverse interest groups sweet simultaneously: the history of London archaeology is simply the long, drawn-out battle which attempts to achieve that goal.

To say that all the odds were stacked against the archaeologist when our story begins would be something of an understatement. In 1840 for example, the Corporation of London devised a road-widening scheme, the principal purpose of which was to destroy the premises of one Charles Roach Smith, an assiduous collector of Roman antiquities. His crime was that he had criticised the Corporation for their pronounced reluctance to take a serious interest in the archaeology of their City. Roach Smith was the founding father of rescue archaeology in London. From 1834 to 1855 he made it his business to watch the very extensive sewer excavation programme in which the City authorities were currently engaged. He records in his magnificent book, *Illustrations of Roman London*, that '... such circumstances were not of themselves the most congenial to an antiquarian explorer ... even if the Corporation of London had thought fit to employ a dozen antiquarians to watch the excavations, the watchers would have been severely tasked. But the Corporation was not embarrassed by any such solicitude.' He eventually sold his magnificent collection to the British Museum (some may still be seen in the Romano-British gallery there), since the Corporation could not be persuaded to purchase it.

The destruction of the remains of the Roman town which lay beneath the modern City continued, as new banks and offices required ever deeper basements. Until 1928, no official body accepted responsibility for the recording of archaeological evidence that was being destroyed, not central Government, the local authority nor the developers themselves. Subsequently the burden has passed from one to the other, with the holders responding with reactions ranging from modest disinterest to realistic support. The initiative was initially taken by the Society of

Antiquaries who, from 1928 to 1937, appointed an Investigator of Building Excavations in London, a post held with distinction by Gerald Dunning (3) and later by Frank Cottrill. However, this was at best salvage archaeology, the recording of what was exposed or collected by workmen hand-digging foundation trenches and the retrieval of finds from the disturbed ground. The site workers who recovered artefacts would eagerly await the arrival of private dealers such as one G. F. Lawrence, who would pay a shilling (twelve old pence) for their finds: the Guildhall Museum officer, on the other hand, was affectionately known as 'Old Tu'pny', since he could only afford to offer them two old pence for

3 *Gerald Dunning was appointed by the Society of Antiquaries as the Investigator of Building Excavations in London from 1929 to 1934. Armed with walking stick and trilby, he inspects Roman quay timbers on the Regis House site, near London Bridge* (Museum of London).

their discoveries. This then was the state of archaeology in the nation's capital: the very idea of mounting a controlled, scientific archaeological excavation in advance of the redevelopment was not even under consideration.

The City suffered terrible damage in the Blitz of 1940–5, for almost one third of the area within the line of the Roman wall was destroyed and much would lie undeveloped for several years. The war had therefore provided an uncalled for but unprecedented opportunity to mount a campaign of research excavations over a substantial sample of the City. The Roman and Medieval Excavation Council was established to instigate this programme. The impetus for the work came not from the Guildhall Museum or the Corporation, but from the Society of Antiquaries and the London Museum who appointed their Keeper, W.F. Grimes, as Director of the project (4). He was an outstanding draughtsman and was considered by many to be the most

4 *Professor W. F. Grimes directed the Roman & Medieval London Excavation Council fieldwork 1946–62. Here he records the Temple of Mithras in September 1954 with Audrey Williams, wearing the woollen hat* (Museum of London).

accomplished excavator of his generation.

The Council began its operations in earnest in July 1947 and worked without ceasing, winter and summer, until December 1962, as its Director recalled in his remarkable report, *The Excavation of Roman and Medieval London*. This was the first chapter in the scientifically-based study of the capital. The resources which he had to call on upon were embarrassingly meagre when compared with the task which faced him, for he was only able to maintain a team of four to five workers moving slowly but methodically from site to cheerless site. During that period, he spent on average less than £3000 per annum on his programme, at a time when workmen's wages rose from £6 to £12 per week. Next to no funds at all were available for post excavation research. Although Grimes records many acts of kindness from individuals within the Corporation, the indifference of the Corporation as a body was a bitter disappointment and a major check on the effectiveness of his programme. There was co-operation with the Guildhall Museum, however, for it undertook the responsibility of the finds from his excavations. Nevertheless, it was the Ministry of Works, the forerunner of English Heritage, which ultimately bore the brunt of the excavation costs.

The grand strategy was to cut a series of trenches on bomb sites right across the City to provide a sample sequence of London's development. While the initial choice of site was therefore made by the Luftwaffe, the actual decision to excavate was determined by the nature of the debris filling the cellar. Without recourse to heavy machinery, some sites simply had to be passed over. The number of controlled excavations conducted during this austere period within and upon the City wall was 53, although many of these were but modest trenches. To this total may be added the discovery of Roman levels beneath St Bride's church to the west of the City in 1952, and beneath St Mary Aldermanbury in 1968. Nevertheless, the value of that work was out of all proportion to its cost, for this was the very first concerted attempt to understand the early development of the City based upon the results of a series of archaeological excavations. Sequences of activity were established, a hitherto unknown fort was discovered at Cripplegate and the infamous temple of Mithras was recorded in the full glare of publicity as 30,000 Londoners looked on. By the end of 1962, his programme of controlled excavations had laid a sound and solid base upon which future research could be built. Although the way forward had been so clearly signposted, not for the first and certainly not for the last time, support for London's archaeology then moved backwards fast.

After 1949, the Corporation's Guildhall Museum paid the salary of one Excavation Assistant, whose job was to monitor all redevelopment work in the City single-handed. This was even more unrealistic than it had been before the war, for now there was not only more rebuilding work, but increasing use of mechanised digging machinery rather than manual labour to move the earth (**5**). One person working on

his own can do little more than buy or beg finds collected by workmen, or retrieve material from spoil heaps while making hurried notes, and obviously can only monitor one project at a time. Such stratigraphic excavation as might be mounted would be banished to the edges of the site and to week-ends. That relations between the Guildhall Museum assistants and the site developers were sometimes strained is to be expected. Museum staff were not the only archaeological contractors on site: at Bucklersbury House for example, freelance archaeologists such as Frances Greenway d'Aquila and son excavated material and lodged their finds with the British Museum. However, it is sadder to note that relations between some of the Guildhall team and the RMLEC were also not always harmonious: both bodies were competing in different ways for increased funding from a begrudging Corporation.

With the conclusion of Professor Grimes's work in 1962, there was but one official archaeologist at work in London. This was Peter

5 *Ivor Noel-Hume was the Guildhall Museum's Excavation Assistant 1950–7. Here he labours alone on the huge St Swithin's House site while Londoners look on* (Museum of London).

Marsden, who had been appointed by the Guildhall Museum the previous year to take on the post previously held by such stalwarts as Adrian Oswald and Ivor Noel-Hume. He continued with the use of volunteers to support the work (their value had been recognised on museum sites since 1949) and, following the dramatic weekend excavation of part of a major bath-house near Huggin Hill in 1964, the City of London Archaeological Society was established (**6**). This was an amateur group who gave up their weekends and holidays to record as much of Londinium as their enthusiasm would allow. The work on the Roman building on the Old Coal Exchange site in Billingsgate and the recording of the second-century ship wreck near Blackfriars Bridge are two of the major projects from this period. There was no official support for his work, beyond such grants as those made in 1966-7 by the Corporation's Engineers and Architects Departments to clear obstructions from sites near the Old Bailey, Aldgate and Billingsgate.

To the credit of Peter Marsden and the volunteer teams, much was rescued in these lean years. Nevertheless, far more was lost than found, since the dice was so heavily weighted against the few. As Peter Marsden himself wrote, 'the years up to 1972 now seem like a bad dream, with missed opportunities and the ruthless destruction of large parts of Roman London'.

A way forward was revealed in 1968, when the first rescue excavation conducted in London by a full-time team of archaeologists took place. This was on a large site astride the south-east corner of the Roman forum near Fenchurch Street. Since the Guildhall Museum's Excavation Assistant was already fully stretched monitoring other sites, a team of excavators from Kent was brought in, led by Brian Philp. Once it became clear what such an organisation could do when supported by funds from the Department of the Environment (formerly the Ministry of Works) and the Corporation, professional teams were then seasonally employed in 1972–3 on sites at Aldgate and Custom House for example. The

6 *By 1964, when Peter Marsden was the Guildhall Museum's Excavation Assistant, a regular band of volunteers gave up their weekends to rescue London's past. The group became known as the City of London Archaeology Society* (Museum of London).

new Director of the Guildhall Museum, Max Hebditch, firmly supported by Ralph Merrifield and Hugh Chapman, had laid the foundations for the next phase in the history of London's archaeology.

A fresh approach

Having thus tested the waters, a full-time team of professional archaeologists was finally established in the City in December of 1973, led by Brian Hobley. The funding for the new Department of Urban Archaeology (DUA) came from the Department of the Environment, initially at a level of £100,000 per annum. At last London had a professional unit dedicated to work in the capital. Excavations could now be mounted all year round on sites threatened by redevelopment, but before the contractors ground works took place (**7**, **8**). Finds could now be processed and researched in quantity while work on the publication of previous investigations could finally begin. This was the culmination of the wishes and dreams of all those who had strived officiously to keep the archaeology of London alive when it seemed in such mortal danger. But would the DUA live up to the expectations of those who had fought so hard to bring it into existence?

Certainly mistakes were made, of which the infamous excavation of the Circle Line in 1974 remains among the most spectacular: the new team had a lot to learn, and learn we did. In its defence, this book summarizes just some of the DUA's work on the Roman town, revealing a part of the potential for detailed research that lies in the Museum's newly garnered excavation archives.

By 1976, when the Guildhall and London Museums were amalgamated to form the new Museum of London, the archaeological team was some 50 strong, and this was subsequently augmented by staff on various Job Creation or Manpower Services Commission projects. The vast conurbation around the City was also provided with archaeological cover with the formation of the Southwark and Lambeth Excavation Committee in 1971 and the Inner London Archaeological Unit in 1974, for example: these units were then brought together with others to

8 *The result of fig. 7: part of the photographic record of the Roman quay at Pudding Lane, near Billingsgate, looking south-east. The 5 x 100mm scale rests on the quay wall, beyond which lies the north face of London's first timber bridge* (Museum of London).

7 *Photographic records: this section of well-preserved first-century quay is being cleaned up before photographs are taken, after which it will be dismantled and destroyed* (Museum of London).

form the Department of Greater London Archaeology (DoGLA) in 1983 under the auspices of the Greater London Council.

There were more gradual but equally profound changes in the funding arrangements for archaeology in the City during the 1980s. Although support for the publication programme was maintained, central government funding for further rescue excavation had been curtailed. Under the government's new philosophy in which 'the polluter pays' 'the developers were now responsible for financing excavations on the sites their redevelopments were destroying. Thus some 34 archaeological investigations were begun within the Square Mile in 1989–90 with a budget of £3,600,000, much of which was provided by the site developers. The City's buried history had never been so well provided for, some felt it would never be so again: a momentous chapter in the rediscovery of Londinium was drawing to a close.

The scale of the work from 1973 to 1991 is arresting, for the DUA excavated as many sites in one year as the RMLEC had achieved in ten. By the end of 1991, tonnes of artefacts had been catalogued, new types of pottery identified and the Museum collections of metal, wooden and leather objects were increased a hundredfold. Hundreds of buildings had been excavated, together with associated pits, ditches, wells and quarries. There were roads, cemeteries, the riverside defensive wall, the eastern half of the Basilica, bath-houses, an amphitheatre, the first-century harbour with its warehouses, wharves and bridge, third-century quays, fourth-century bastions. But above all, sequences of datable activity had been recorded on a wide geographical spread of over 300 sites from which a detailed picture of the complex development of the changing town could be established. It was this fact, rather than any one particularly spectacular discovery, which must stand as the DUA's major contribution to the study of Londinium.

Modus operandi

One of the most common questions asked of the DUA diggers by the interested public observing their work was how did we know where to dig? Techniques such as aerial photography or field walking which are used by rural archaeologists to locate sites are clearly not appropriate for work in an urban centre. For the DUA, the choice of site was quite straight-forward: if it was about to be destroyed, then it would be excavated first. In other words, site selection and the amount of resources allocated to a particular project have been largely determined by the developer rather than a rigid excavation research strategy. As a consequence, a data collection exercise has been implemented in which as many sites and sequences as possible have been sampled as they became 'available', i.e., in advance of their imminent destruction. In this way, we have tried to anticipate the unexpected, by never writing off areas that superficially may have seemed less interesting than others. This non-selective attitude has paid dividends, for we have discovered roads, first-century quays and even an amphitheatre in places were they were not expected.

The *modus operandi* adopted by the DUA ran on these lines. First, all planning applications for developments in the City were vetted by checking the addresses against information in the Museum archive to gain an impression of what archaeological levels might be under threat. Previous work in the area provided data such as the anticipated level of the natural ground surface and the general character of the ancient deposits, while a brief survey of relevant documentary material provided a context for Saxon and later Medieval developments. If after such studies it seemed that the site clearly merited excavation, i.e., all archaeological levels had not been destroyed by previous activity, then negotiations would begin with the developer.

In the early 1970s, such discussions were principally concerned with gaining access for the archaeological teams. Later in that decade and throughout the next, financial support for the work was also requested. A timetable was then arranged in which the archaeological work was dovetailed into the redevelopment programme. At first, the standard procedure was to send the archaeologists in after the old building had been demolished, but before foundation work on the new project began. The archaeologists therefore had sole occupancy of the site for a given period. This meant that the building programme was lengthened, rather than delayed, by the Museum work. But it soon became commonplace for the DUA to excavate in the cellars of standing buildings before demolition took place (9), either while the last of the tenants sat out the residue of their lease or as soft-stripping of the fabric on the upper floors took place. By such schemes, the archaeologists could be seen to be refuting the age-old allegation that they added unnecessary costs to the programme by delaying redevelopments. Indeed, as construction programmes became ever more complex, not to say hectic in the 1980s and 90s, ever more theoretically ingenious solutions were devised to squeeze the archaeologists into the works schedule: on one site at 22–3 Birchin Lane, for example, the team worked in round-the-clock

9 *In house: many recent archaeological excavations have been conducted indoors, before the building was demolished or refurbished. Here archaeologists work below the floor of the Coleman Street Ward School gymnasium in 1981. Modern excavations are as much concerned with civil engineering as with Roman London* (Museum of London).

shifts to get the work done. We were frequently obliged to dig on one part of the site while piling rigs drilled next to us or construction work began behind, around or over us. We no longer had the luxury of the sole occupancy of a site, but had to share it with heavy machinery going about its noisy business and sub-contractors on piece-work with, at best, a rudimentary knowledge of safety legislation.

A number of shafts and tunnels have been dug through prime archaeological deposits beneath London's streets, and these too have had to be recorded. In the close confines of a 1m-high telephone cable tunnel, the only recording time is during the tea and lunch breaks taken by the tunnellers. The effort has been well worth it: Roman roads and masonry buildings have been recorded beneath Threadneedle Street, the forum below Gracechurch Street, and a Roman

quay below Thames Street. The work on the shafts for the Docklands Light Railway extension to Bank also proved very profitable, with the archaeologists excavating in tandem with the insertion of the concrete caissons.

Ironically, money for digging became less of an obstacle to the developers in the late 1980s provided their schedules were left intact: although we had the resources to mount the excavation, the time and space to dissect the remains of London's history were severely constrained. Large areas of larger sites were routinely written off with, at best, cursory observations. Monitoring ground reduction by mechanical excavators working at speed to keep a stream of lorries filled (the technical term was 'muck away') is always a daunting task. A watching brief meant precisely that: you watched briefly, not to mention helplessly, as large slices of Roman, Saxon and Medieval London disappeared unrecorded into the back of a lorry (**10**). Many attempts were made to impose some sort of order upon these exercises in salvage archaeology. These ranged from developing the concept of the 'stopping brief', whereby the archaeologists negotiated the right to hold up machine-clearance for limited periods so that a particular feature might be recorded, to searching through the spoil removed from the excavation after it had been dumped elsewhere on a landfill site in Kent or Essex.

That said, the controlled excavation of the sample areas was conducted by the DUA in a way which was just not feasible 20 to 30 years earlier. Each layer or feature was exposed, cleaned, planned, levelled and recorded before being excavated and the associated finds and samples collected. The excavation of each area continued, layer after layer, until the natural ground surface, usually undisturbed orange Brickearth, was exposed. In this way, complete stratified sequences of artefacts and horizons representing the development of London were recovered from hundreds of small trenches or larger areas in almost every parish of the City over the 18-year campaign. A concerted attempt

10 *Watching brief, or spot the archaeologist: machine clearance of the site at Cross Keys Court, near London Wall in 1982. In the top right hand corner, the white-helmeted archaeologists rush to record layers exposed in the section by the mechanical excavators* (Museum of London).

was made to ensure that each of these sequences was recorded in as uniform a manner as was practical, to facilitate comparisons and correlations of data from sites excavated in different years by different teams. After all, we were digging one large site, the much disturbed remains of Londinium, albeit in a series of discrete trenches which needed to be related to be understood.

This is not to say that our recording system remained unchanged, quite the reverse. To meet the particular demands of London archaeology, a flexible system was developed. The standard method of excavation conducted by the RMLEC was in narrow trenches, using the information recorded in the sections to determine the stratigraphic sequence: by 1973, attempts had been made to excavate sites such as that at Aldgate in plan as an open area. Before 1974, recording stratigraphy in London incorporated site note-books

and large multi-layer phase plans. These primary field records were usually compiled by the site supervisors or their assistants, and not by the excavators actually revealing the layers. As the new London teams rapidly gained experience, a new system was developed which entailed the use of individual context sheets and individual plans for each layer or feature (**11**), compiled by the excavators themselves as they excavated. The role of the DUA supervisor therefore changed to one of keeping the work programme on schedule and ensuring that the records were completed consistently and comprehensively. This new work pattern was ideally suited to the London environment, where the archaeological levels were often divided into discrete islands by later pits and foundation trenches. Using the improved system, the excavation and recording of each discrete island could continue at the pace dictated by the complexity of the deposits and the skill of the excavators. However, such a seemingly disparate excavation methodology demands that the records are related to a single stratigraphic framework for the site as a whole, and to achieve this each context number and each plan number had to be entered on the site matrix tables which show which layers are earlier or later than others.

The integration of the individual sequences recorded on each site would not be resolved until the field work had finished, when the records could be collated during the compilation of the archive report. This represents a crucial stage in the understanding of the site, for it entails reconstructing the entire site sequence on paper, using the unique context plans to build up each phase from the earliest layers to the latest. Such a procedure is the reverse of the excavation process, and seems the only sensible way to understand a complex sequence of urban deposits.

Finds study

Meanwhile, the finds staff processed the pottery, building material, metalwork and animal bone (**12**). The material had to be washed, marked, weighed, computerised and catalogued before serious study could begin. The preliminary

dating and assessment of the artefacts gave a date range for the site: the excavator would then know whether the sequence of buildings just identified represented early, mid or late Roman occupation. Further research might provide evidence for function and status, or for the commercial life of the town. A smithy might be represented by deposits containing slag and a cache of used nails ripe for recycling, a shoe-maker's workshop by leather off-cuts together with leather working tools. Study of the building materials from destruction levels provide important evidence of the status of the demolished houses: the type of flooring, nature of wall plaster, the presence or absence of roof tile all contribute to those interpretations.

11 *Planning an* op. sig. *floor in the nave of the second-century basilica, using a planning frame, plumb bob, pencil and drafting film. Leadenhall Court excavations in 1985* (Museum of London).

12 *When the dig is over, the work begins. A small section of one of the many stores in which artefacts from twenty years' excavation are housed* (Museum of London).

Comparison of the assemblages from several sites has helped identify the focus for the earliest and latest settlement in Londinium, and also the location of residential, industrial and commercial quarters. Important details of mercantile activity can also be illuminated, as Dr Paul Tyers showed in a comparative study of the imported storage jars known as amphoras. Some 77% of the first- and second-century pottery from the quayside sites near Billingsgate were from amphoras, a figure which is double the percentage from contemporary domestic sites away from the waterfront. This neatly highlights the particular interests and activities of the harbour area. However, he was also able to show that sherds from the globular Dressel 20 olive oil amphora were widespread throughout the City, in contrast to the cylindrical storage jars for Italian wine and Spanish fish sauce, which had a more restricted distribution. He suggests that olive oil was therefore widely used by the majority of the population, whereas some of the other imported products of the wider Roman world were only enjoyed by the more prosperous or more Romanized citizens. Comparison of the first and second-century pottery groups with the later

material was also instructive, since it demonstrates that the range and quantity of material imported into Londinium had changed considerably during the Roman period. The large 'mercantile' assemblages characteristic of the early Roman waterfront sites are not found in the late third and fourth centuries, which supports the suggestion that London was not a major port or redistribution centre during the later Empire.

End of an era

In the 1980s the Corporation had adopted a planning policy for the City in which were enshrined the following principles: the prevention of the destruction of potentially valuable archaeological remains when sites are redeveloped; support for every opportunity for the investigation and recording of archaeological sites; the safeguarding of important archaeological remains. The Corporation had moved a long way since the days of Charles Roach Smith and was now providing solid support for London's archaeology. So too were the developers following a major breakthrough in 1986, when a voluntary Code of Conduct had been drawn up by archaeologists and the British Property Federation 'to achieve a realistic understanding between archaeologists and developers' so that sites and funds would be made available for excavations.

By 1990 it would seem that everything was falling into place: London's archaeology seemed to be enjoying the support of the Museum, the developers and the Corporation. Even the Department of the Environment was falling into line (following problems over the Rose Theatre and Huggin Hill bath-house sites), with the drafting of *Planning Policy Guidance Note 16: archaeology and planning*, known in the trade as PPG16. This influential document made it known that, where archaeological sites were threatened by re-development, 'there should be a presumption in favour of preservation' but, if rebuilding was to go ahead and archaeological excavations were needed to record the threatened levels, then the DoE 'considered it reasonable for developers to contribute towards the cost' of such excavation.

However, September 1990 marked the beginning of the end of the DUA, with the issue of the first round of redundancies: much of the team had been dispersed by the end of 1991, victims of a deep and sudden recession which stopped redevelopment dead in its tracks, leaving the City with an alarming over-provision of office space. In December 1991, the two major London units, the DUA and DoGLA, closed down and a smaller Museum of London Archaeological Service (MoLAS) was set up in their stead. The new unit is financially independent of the Museum, and has to cover all the costs for the work it is contracted to do by the charges it makes. It provides developers with an evaluation service, whereby the archaeologists establish the extent of the ancient remains threatened by rebuilding before redevelopment begins. In keeping with current planning legislation, the destruction of the Roman levels can therefore be limited or even avoided, as can the need for extensive, expensive controlled excavation. This new presumption in favour of preservation means that the scale of archaeological oppor-

tunity presented to the DUA from 1973 to 1991 may never be seen again. MoLAS now has a team of some 150, which some would consider too small to cope with the excavation and research of the nation's capital and surrounding area. That is a measure of how much attitudes have changed over the last twenty years, or indeed the last century: there had been a time when the Corporation of London had seen even one archaeologist as one too many.

The quest for Londinium has therefore passed from the Society of Antiquaries, to the Roman and Medieval London Excavation Council; from the London Museum to the Guildhall Museum and then to the Museum of London's Department of Urban Archaeology: its funding has come from the Ministry of Works, later the Department of the Environment and subsequently English Heritage, and latterly from the generosity of a pantheon of property developers: it has thus been through the hands of enthusiastic amateurs and hardened professionals as well as the vagaries of market forces. In sum, London archaeology is as much a reflection of the politics of the day as it is a means of understanding our past.

3
Dating the data

In Britain, the Roman military occupation lasted from AD 43 to c. 410, while many would argue that a recognisably Roman way of life persisted in many parts of the province until at least c. AD 450. Thus the Roman period in this country was some 400 years long, during which time Britannia saw almost as many changes as beset England from 1600 to the present day. For many of the early antiquaries, it was enough to describe a newly-discovered mosaic or pottery fragment simply as 'Roman'. That process simply served to identify the object as older then medieval but is too imprecise a term to facilitate detailed interpretation in so long an era. The recording of an ancient feature is not itself enough: it needs to be closely dated before it can be understood and before implications for its social context can be drawn. Archaeologists need to know precisely when a building was built before they begin to wonder why.

Absolute (or calendar) dating also provides the means whereby features found on different sites in different years can be sensibly compared one with another. However, the increasing precision with which Roman levels can now be dated should lead directly to a clearer understanding of the associated developments. For example, a later chapter presents evidence for a major re-planning of Londinium in AD 85, differentiating that scheme from the redevelopments of AD 70. The point to be stressed here is that it is now possible to consider posing questions which identify construction phases ten to fifteen years

apart: such precision is a measure of the progress made by archaeological research since 1973.

From relative to absolute dating

One of the most significant contributions to the study of Londinium which the work of the DUA achieved was the recording of so many stratified sequences, representing layer upon layer of Roman activity. As a consequence, a comprehensive framework of relatively-dated events and features in many parts of the City was established, following the rigorous stratigraphic analysis of the field records from each site. Broad calendar dates were then imposed upon parts or all of those relative sequences by the use of such methodologies as dendrochronology, the examination of ceramics, or coins, all three of which are summarised below. On many sites the pottery evidence provides a broad date range for the occupation represented, while the coins or dendrochronology are used to refine that picture. Other classes of material can also be used to help date features from Roman London, such as types of tile, brick, mosaic floor or painted wall-plaster known to have been used in a particular period, or a range of copper alloy and glass artefacts which can be compared with examples of known date found elsewhere. Radiocarbon dating was attempted on the riverside wall excavation at Baynard's Castle in 1975, but that methodology has sometimes proved too imprecise for our increasingly particular demands.

Dating our Roman sites does not rely,

therefore, on the study of just one class of artefact, but considers the evidence from all quarters, related to the stratigraphic analysis. Perhaps the most spectacular method of dating London excavations is the identification of the infamous Boudican fire horizon within a site sequence. Such a layer might comprise a spread of burnt mud-brick, daub or charcoal representing the remains of buildings from the first Roman settlement destroyed during the native revolt against the occupying powers in AD 61. Such a horizon would appear close to the bottom of the Roman occupation sequence and, if correctly identified, provides us with a means of dating the buildings destroyed, the levels beneath them (which must date to the years *before* AD 61) and the levels immediately above them, which must consequently be dated to the years *after* that unhappy episode. Thus such historical dating provides some absolute dates for three horizons at once. Unfortunately there are few other events in the calendar of Roman London which have left such a readily-identifiable impression. Although clear evidence for several later fires has been recorded on many recent sites, it is often difficult to be certain whether a major London-wide conflagration is represented which can be tied down to a particular date. A case can be made for a substantial and extensive fire sometime between 120 and 130, an event which Gerald Dunning in 1945 termed the 'Hadrianic Fire'. There is no corroborative historical evidence to support this suggestion however, so we cannot be certain that a single calamity was responsible for all of the early to mid second-century destruction horizons recorded on recent sites or whether several discrete, localised and unconnected events occurred. To sum up: there is only one readily identifiable datable historical event commonly represented in the archaeological record of Roman London, the Boudican revolt of AD 61, although the considerable evidence for a second-century conflagration is often used as a second major bench mark in the dating of Roman sites, particularly on sites in the western half of the City. Given the limitations of

13 *Roman coin photographed in 1985. It was lying where it fell in the mortar beneath the second-century basilica* (Museum of London).

'historical' dating, it is clear that, if the development of Londinium is to be dated, then the associated artefacts must be studied.

Coins

Until the recent developments in ceramic studies and dendrochronology, the study of coins was the prime dating methodology for Londinium (**13**). Since most official Roman coins carry the head of an emperor and a legend, it is often possible to establish the year in which a given example was minted: thus, unlike most other objects found on archaeological sites, coins are intrinsically datable. There are drawbacks to their use however, as Jenny Hall has shown. Coins are much rarer finds than potsherds, many are often recovered in a corroded condition and thus prove to be unidentifiable, while some prove to have been in circulation for a long time: an extreme example of this was noted on the Leadenhall Court site, where a very worn Republican coin of *c.* 250–150 BC was found in a layer otherwise dated to the first century AD. In spite of such problems, the study of Roman coins has been of major importance in the development of a chronology for Londinium: the dating of the landward wall was determined by coin evidence for example. A slightly worn coin of Commodus (AD 183–4) which was probably lost in about AD 190 was recovered from deposits earlier than the wall, while a small hoard of coins and forger's moulds were found in a tower on the wall. That group cannot have been discarded much before 215–25, since it contained a coin of Caracalla minted in AD 213–17 which was little worn. Thus the city wall was shown to have been built after AD 190 and to have been operative by AD 220; unfortunately not all Roman buildings have such conveniently placed coins associated with them.

Pottery studies

Pottery is the most common find on London sites (**14**). Since certain types are known to have been manufactured at a particular date, whenever such vessels are found in association with a building, then a date range for that structure can be suggested. Ceramic dating is being refined continuously as securely dated groups and kiln sites are studied and published. Although imported finewares like red samian ware have tradi-

tionally been seen as the more readily datable types of pottery, recent research has shown that local wares can also be dated with precision in some circumstances. For example, since the kilns which produced Sugar Loaf Court ware (named after a City site at which kiln debris was found) seemed to have ceased production in AD 60, the presence of such vessels in an assemblage suggest a date in the very first years of the Roman occupation. After AD 60, pottery from the kilns at Highgate, to the north of Londinium, began to be used in the city, while ring-necked flagons made near Verulamium were introduced shortly after AD 70. The ubiquitous Black Burnished wares from southern England were introduced here after AD 110, Oxfordshire colour-coated vessels not before the late third century, while Portchester D-ware is only found in deposits of late fourth-century date or later.

There had been little attempt at a systematic

14 *Pottery is the most common find on archaeological sites in London. Differences in the form, fabric and type can be used to date it* (Museum of London).

study of Roman pottery in London before the 1970s, and it is a tribute to the work of Dr Paul Tyers and Geoff Marsh, and subsequently to Barbara Davies and Beth Richardson, that the situation now has much improved. The last ten years have seen even greater changes, as computerisation has revolutionised the study of London's Roman pottery since 1981 (**15**). Instead of re-examining the ceramics themselves, a provisional date can now be established for any layer or feature just by examining computer lists which record the size of the assemblage and the pottery fabrics and forms represented. The finds from over 250 sites have now been computerised, and the study of that data has shown that the presence, absence or proportions of particular forms and fabrics formed consistent patterns in groups of a similar date. These patterns have been studied in detail on the large well-stratified groups of pottery from such sites as the Newgate Street excavation, from the Walbrook valley, in the harbour area, and more recently, on the Basilica site at Leadenhall Court. As a consequence, it proved possible to identify and develop a series of six 'ceramic phases' for the period between AD 50–150. The suggested dating for these phases is:

RCP 1A:	*c.* AD 50–60/1
RCP 1B:	*c.* AD 60/1–70
RCP 2:	*c.* AD 70–100
RCP 3:	*c.* AD 100–20
RCP 4:	*c.* AD 120–40
RCP 5:	*c.* AD 140–60

It proved possible to identify significant patterns in the material broadly dated to the late first century, as a consequence of which RCP2 could now be split into two to make seven ceramic phases for the early Roman period.

Unfortunately the study of London's later Roman pottery is not as well advanced, although important work has been done on the large early third-century group from St Magnus House waterfront (**16**), on the late Roman sequence from Leadenhall Court, on the coin-dated groups from Dowgate Hill House and the Roman bath-house

15 *Computers revolutionised pottery studies in London. The new technology as it looked in 1983* (Museum of London).

in Lower Thames Street. Although a clearly-defined framework of Roman ceramic phases has not, as yet, been imposed upon the later period, broad patterns have now been identified between AD 200 and 270, 270 and 350, and after AD 350.

Tree ring studies: building the reference chronology for Roman London

The application of tree-ring studies to samples of well-preserved Roman wood from London excavations is potentially one of the most important advances in the development of a chronology for that town. Large areas of the City contain waterlogged deposits from which ancient timbers have been recovered. These include the zone next to the Thames (it was on the Roman quay on the Custom House site in this zone that dendrochronology was first used in London in 1973), the wide Walbrook valley in the centre of the City and the Fleet Valley just to the west of the town wall. However, there is a relatively high water table over much of the rest of the intramural area and as a consequence the bases of timber-lined wells and wooden drains have been

16 *Part of the huge assemblage of Samian ware pottery imported from Gaul (France) recovered from a third-century waterfront site in 1974–5* (Museum of London).

recorded on many sites. Even though the amphitheatre lies on a hill-top site high above the Thames waterfront, the lower levels of that excavation contained well-preserved timbers from which dendrochronological dates were obtained.

The principles upon which dendrochronology relies are based on the simple principle that trees such as oak grow a new layer each year during the spring and summer. These layers, when seen in cross section, form the pattern of more or less concentric circles termed annual rings, and thus a 95-year-old tree will have 95 rings. The width of each ring will be determined by environ-

mental conditions prevalent during the growing season, with adverse conditions such as drought producing narrow rings, for example. Distinctive patterns of narrow and wide rings on an excavated sample can thus be identified and matched with similar patterns recorded in an established, dated reference chronology. These were initially based on work in Germany, but chronologies are now available for England, Ireland and Scotland. If the full complement of rings survives in the sample being matched, that is all the heartwood, sapwood and even the bark, then a felling date which is accurate to the year may be proposed for the tree from which the sample was derived: e.g., AD 84. Unfortunately, the bark and the outermost rings (which include the sapwood) were often removed in antiquity when the timber was cut and squared for use and so absolutely precise felling dates are all too rarely obtained. In such cases it may nevertheless be possible to suggest a felling date range if some of the sapwood rings survive, since oak trees are unlikely to have less than 10 or more than 55 sapwood rings: a sample with 20 sapwood rings may be given a felling date range of AD 63–98 for example. However, if all the pattern identified on the heartwood rings can be matched but there are no sapwood rings at all on a sample, then the best date that can be suggested is, for example, AD 51+, which means unequivocally not before but sometime after (perhaps long after) AD 51.

The development of the dendrochronology of Roman London has been described by Jennifer Hillam of the Sheffield University Dendrochronological Laboratory which was set up in 1975 by the agency which is now known as English Heritage. She was responsible for measuring most of the London samples, although Dr Fletcher of Oxford University had attempted to

date material from the Custom House site previously. By 1980, work on medieval samples had been extended back into the Roman period, and an English chronology spanning the years AD 404 to 1216 had been established. Meanwhile, samples from the Seal House and St Magnus House and Thames Street Tunnel quay sites had been matched with timbers from the inland sites at Watling Court and Milk Street to produce a long floating chronology. A computer programme developed in Belfast by Dr Baillie enabled that sequence to be matched against dated German material as well as an Irish

17 *On waterlogged sites where wood survives, dendrochronologists can estimate felling dates for timbers incorporated in structures such as this early third-century quay. This example was recorded on the Thames Exchange site in 1989: the piles of a multi-storey carpark just missed it in 1960. The view is looking north-east, away from the river. The 5 x 100mm scale sits on the front wall, the 10 x 10mm scale on a severed brace* (Museum of London).

sequence extending back to 13 BC. Thus an absolutely-dated chronology for Roman London was established by 1981, running from 252 BC to AD 209. To this, timbers from the Roman quays at Pudding Lane were added, after which the Museum of London's own dendrochronological team began work led by Ian Tyers. The London sequence was then extended to AD 255 and, by 1985, to AD 294 with the samples from St Peter's Hill site. Since then, although timbers from more quay excavations have been examined (**17**), no samples have been found which extend the sequence into the fourth century, and a gap in the Roman London reference chronology of 110 years, from AD 294 to AD 404, still needs to be filled.

Dendrochronological study can therefore provide absolute, independent dating for timber samples under certain conditions. These conditions were met with great success on the St Peter's Hill site, where piles from an enigmatic masonry structure were shown to have been felled in AD 293, 294 and 295. This was the period when the usurper Allectus was governing the province, and presumably undertaking major building programmes before his death in 296: significantly, his London project was unfinished. In addition, it has been used to determine the period of time between two phases of activity, as in the case of the first-century landing stage on the Pudding Lane site which was superseded by an infilled quay structure. Examination of samples from both the timber structures showed that the landing stage could only have been operative for no more than 15 years before it was replaced. Another crucial attribute of dendrochronological study is the facility to compare dates for structures on different, often widely-separated sites. Thus piles from beneath different sections of the mile-long late Roman riverside wall were shown to have been cut at different dates, showing that the wall was not built in one

brisk campaign, for example.

As has been mentioned, work on constructing the London reference chronologies continues, which means that samples which cannot be dated today may meet with more success tomorrow, and so should not be discarded. Two important examples of this maxim may be mentioned, both concerning samples from Roman boats which Ian Tyers studied in 1991. The Blackfriars I wreck was excavated in 1962-3, ten years before any dendrochronological work had been attempted in London on Roman material. Nevertheless, some of the dried-out planks from the wreck have now been re-examined, and were found to have come from trees felled between AD 130–75. Even more remarkable was the recent work on timbers recovered from the County Hall wreck, discovered in 1910 which was 20 years before dendrochronology itself was invented. Some 90 years after the excavation, samples from planks preserved with linseed oil and tar were measured. They were cut from trees felled some time after AD 277, and might suggest that the vessel was constructed in the late 280s, perhaps when Carausius had been appointed commander of the British fleet.

This summary has shown that a number of methodologies are now available to the London archaeologist eager to date a site sequence. However, it must be stressed that the essential starting point is a clear understanding of the stratigraphic sequence, providing a framework within which the associated features are relatively dated. Once that is established, the use of a combination of methodologies can lead to ever greater precision. A site or building which has been securely dated can then be profitably compared with contemporary sites in London and elsewhere. Dating is therefore a means to an end without which meaningful research into London's past cannot sensibly begin.

4

An undistinguished settlement?

The first goals of our archaeological study were to determine when, where and how the city was born, whether or not a more ancient settlement preceded it and what the site looked like before the Roman town was founded. The blueprint for the DUA's programme, the survey by Martin Biddle, *The Future of London's Past*, presented the options for the birth of the city: was there, for example, a Conquest-period fort beneath London which provided the focus for its later development, or was it a civilian town founded by merchants? The closer the foundation date was to AD 43, so the argument ran, the more likely was the military solution. In addition we needed to know what form the new town took, when its streets were first established, how regular that street plan was. The more formal the layout, the more official sanction the new town might have enjoyed: conversely, an irregular, haphazard plan might suggest a less-regulated organic growth. And finally, how extensive was the occupied area on the eve of its destruction in the Boudican revolt of AD 61? This was the Londinium described by Tacitus as 'not distinguished by the title of "colonia" ': how undistinguished was the settlement which would later serve as the provincial capital?

London before Londinium

Our enquiry began by using a wide range of evidence to build up a picture of the natural topography and vegetation of the area. As a consequence of this palaeo-ecological study coupled with a detailed contour survey, we can now appreciate why Londinium was sited precisely where it was. Surprisingly, the answer lay not so much on the steeply-rising north bank beneath the modern day City, but in the river channel itself and on the southern shore, in Southwark. In the Roman period, this was low-lying land with a series of islands separated by marsh and mud flats, and between which the braided channels of the Thames ran. Samples taken from first-century foreshore deposits contained microscopic algae know as diatoma. Of the varieties represented, one of the more significant was *Cyclotella striata*, a type commonly found in the brackish water of estuaries. This shows that the river must have been tidal as far west as London at this period, contrary to the conclusions of some earlier studies. It was also possible to suggest what the tidal range might be. At low tide, the river must have dropped to more than c. 1m (3ft) below Ordnance Datum (OD = mean sea level) since first-century quarry pits had been dug to that level in the foreshore to extract London Clay. However, the tide cannot have been expected to rise more than 1.5m (5ft) above OD, since this was the level of the lowest operative surface of the first Roman roads laid in Southwark. For comparison, present day high tides can be higher than +4.5m (15ft) OD, with a tidal range of up to 7.7m (25ft). Clearly, the river level has changed considerably over the last 2000 years.

Having established the tidal values for AD 50,

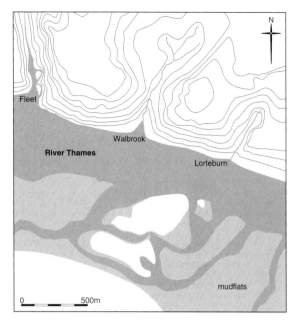

18 Natural topography: the contours, rivers, streams and islands that lie beneath the modern city. The extent of the Thames is shown at low tide in the first century, with mudflats exposed on the southern shore (Chrissie Milne).

the width of the river at high and low tide was then calculated by plotting the relevant contours on both banks (**18**). The problems which faced the Roman engineers who were considering bridging the Thames then became evident and the crucial importance of the Southwark islands obvious. At high tide, the Thames was up to 1000m wide in places, whereas at low tide it was some 300m across at its narrowest point, which was where the largest island projected into the deep water channel. It was there and only there that the lowest crossing could be made by a fixed bridge. Thus it was not the favoured high ground on the north bank which determined where the City should stand, but the real constraints on the southern shore: Southwark's island topography dictated where the roads and the river crossing and therefore, by extension, where the City itself should be built.

On the north bank, much of Londinium was built on deposits of gravel sealed by Brickearth, an orange-brown clay-like silt which, as its name suggests, was extensively quarried for the mak-

ing of bricks. A systematic logging of all exposures of this material in the City, whether on archaeological excavations, in boreholes or in trenches dug in the road for cables and pipes, has shown that the terrace on the north bank of the Thames rose to the modest heights of 12m (39ft) or so above sea level. This plateau was cut by several valleys, of which the two largest were for the River Fleet in the west (on the line of the present-day road leading to Blackfriars Bridge) and the Walbrook stream, which together with its numer-ous tributaries, drained southwards into the Thames in the centre of the City, the confluence being close to what is now Cannon Street Station. A third valley, that of the Lorteburn stream, has been identified running southwards from the site of Fenchurch Street Station beneath Seething Lane.

The valleys therefore formed the boundaries of the two hills upon which Londinium was built: Ludgate Hill to the west, crowned today by St Paul's, Cornhill to the east, dominated by the Nat West tower: God and mammon. The contours and course of those ancient rivers are now infilled and obscured by a thick blanket of buildings and centuries of redevelopment. However, those streams were of some significance in defining the size and extent of the first town, for most of the original settlement seems to have been confined to the area between the Walbrook and the Lorteburn valleys. Thus the position of first settlement was determined by an island in Southwark, while its extent was initially confined to a readily defensible position with river valleys to east and west (**19**).

Although these rivers are no longer visible, it is possible to describe what they looked like 2000 years ago. The tributaries of the Walbrook for example have been extensively studied in recent excavations, the course of the channels plotted, and samples from the sediments and silts examined. From these, remains of plants, insects, molluscs and ostracods have all been identified. Since these all have preferences for a particular type of environment, a detailed picture of the contemporary conditions can be drawn. For

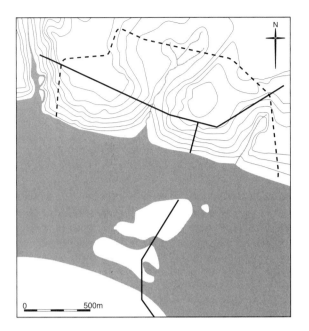

19 *This plan shows how the line of the Roman wall and some of the main axial roads relate to the natural topography. The Thames is shown at high tide in the first century, with the mud flats marked on fig. **18** now covered* (Chrissie Milne).

example, the most recent study of material from the earliest levels suggests that the stream was fairly free – but not fast-flowing – ran through a natural marshy area and its water was clean and clear. The evidence was based on the discovery of seeds from plants whose presence indicates marshland, while aquatic plants included stonewort, horned pondweed and watercress. The identification of freshwater snails such as *Lymnaea stagnalis* shows that the river did not dry up seasonally while the presence of ostracods such as *Ilyocypris bradyi* indicates that the water was unpolluted. Since the insect assemblage contained no varieties which are associated with the activities of man (such as grain beetles), it seems that this particular area was not settled in the pre-Roman period. Samples from later levels graphically demonstrated how Roman developments detrimentally altered this environment.

A prehistoric settlement?

As for the origins of the town, the last twenty years' excavation have done nothing to substantiate the ancient medieval tradition of a town founded by Brutus in 1108 BC and called New Troy, or the one walled and towered by King Lud called Caer Lud in Julius Ceasar's time. However, finds of flints and prehistoric pottery have been made from time to time on the site of the later City. To the detailed list recently discussed by Dr Merriman can be added flints from 2 Seething Lane and 6 Austin Friars, the Late Bronze Age–Early Iron pottery from sites at 41 Bishopsgate, 58 Gracechurch Street, Giltspur Street, St Martin Orgar and St Mary-at-Hill, and the Iron Age pottery from Finsbury Circus. Much of this material was actually recovered from sealed features, but next to none of it *directly* pre-dates the Roman settlement.

Taken together with the other features such as the pre-Roman burial within the precinct of the Tower, there is clearly a body of prehistoric material well worth studying in its own right. Nevertheless, our extensive campaigns seem to have shown that, even if there may have been an isolated farm or set of fields, there was certainly no substantial Iron Age oppidum lying beneath the first-century town on the north bank. Interestingly, there is even more evidence of pre-Roman occupation on the supposedly less illustrious southern shore. Recent work in Southwark has revealed traces of round houses and occupation debris dating to the middle-to-late Iron Age, but even these seem to represent a sequence of dispersed farmsteads rather than a nucleated settlement. Whatever the real meaning of the obscure Celtic word *Londinio* might prove to be, it presumably made reference to a natural feature rather than to a large Iron Age town, hill fort or other settlement centre. London was indeed a Roman creation, set, not in the heart of a tribal district, but at the very boundary of several ancient kingdoms. It lay on the no-man's land between the Catuvellauni and Trinovantes to the north, and the Atrebates and Cantii to the south. For those people, the Thames seems to have been a barrier; for the Romans it became a highway.

Thames crossing

The Roman invasion of Britain in AD 43 was ruthless but protracted. The legions which landed on the south-east coast near Richborough battled their way up to and over the Thames, then made for the ancient centre of population and power of the celtic tribes at Camulodunum (Colchester). From the fortress they established there, attacks were launched northwards and westwards, linking with other landings on the coast. In the wake of the military advance, roads and supply lines were laid out, settlements were established. One such was Londinium, built on the banks of the Thames at a junction with the new road network. In this early period the town seems to have been served by a ferry, since no evidence of a contemporary permanent bridge has yet been recovered. A landing place on the foreshore may be represented by a flint and chalk surface recorded on the Pudding Lane site, close to the site of the later bridge. The town therefore seems to have grown up opposite this Thames ferry crossing and along the main east–west Roman road. It was a supply base at an important junction in the evolving Roman communications network: it lay at the head of an important Thames crossing initially served by a ferry, with the main road to the channel ports to the south, the road to the capital at Colchester to the east, and the roads to the active military frontier to north and west. Food, goods and equipment destined for the army could be brought here by road from Richborough or upriver by boat, and then transferred as required by land to the front line.

However, dating evidence from sites north and south of the City–Southwark crossing suggests that Roman settlement began sometime *after* AD 50, that is after the legions had left their fortress at Camulodunum and it had been converted into the first capital of the Roman province of Britannia. This implies that the initial Roman crossing of the Thames which carried the traffic from the channel coast to the new frontier was not at London but elsewhere: a strong contender must be at Westminster where the river is shallower and narrower opposite Thorney Island, where the Houses of Parliament now stand. Traces of two first-century roads have been recorded on the south bank near the later bridge, one of which seemed to be heading in the direction of a Westminster crossing. Later work has not confirmed the route and it now seems likely that that second road was constructed simply to provide access to the south-western corner of the island upon which it was laid. If there was a main route to the Westminster area, then it most likely followed the edge of the higher land to the south of the Southwark islands.

Fast birth: quick death

In AD 60, with the southern part of the country ostensibly subdued, the full force of the Roman military machine was directed at the celtic tribes in North Wales. At that moment a revolt broke out in what is now East Anglia, led by Boudica, queen of the Iceni. Although it was finally put down with standard Roman severity, a contemporary reference records that at least three major settlements had been destroyed: one of them was Londinium, and thus the first mention of that new town in our written records is on the eve of its destruction, as noted in Chapter 1.

As for the archaeological records of the settlement at that momentous time, there have been considerable advances. Something of its extent, foundation date and origins, its street grid, its buildings and the traffic and trade which passed through it have all been learned (**20**). The evidence for this phase of the town comes principally from sites upon which graphic evidence of the Boudican revolt has been recovered, often in the form of a readily-identifiable horizon of burnt building debris associated with or sealing artefacts and coins dated to the period AD 50–60. As long ago as 1945, Gerald Dunning suggested that Cornhill, the eastern of London's two hills, had been the primary focus for the settlement, since more burnt Roman samian pottery of that date had been found on building sites there than to the west. That view has been supported and

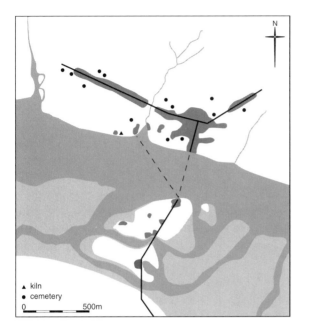

20 *Londinium in* AD *55. This plan shows the approximate extent of the early settlement, shown in the darker tone (not all streets are marked). The town may have been served by ferries rather than by a bridge in this phase* (Chrissie Milne).

extended by subsequent excavation. Material dating to *c.* AD 50–60 has been recovered from Fish Street Hill, Clements Lane and Fenchurch Street in the south to Cullum Street and Whittington Avenue and even as far north as Bishopsgate. Recent work on a site off Cheapside has shown that the 9m (30ft) wide Roman precursor to that main road was one of the primary features of the settlement and that building erected next to it incorporated timbers felled in AD 53 with a rebuilding phase in AD 59. Such is the precision of dendrochronological research when conditions are favourable. These dates are in accord with those from the settlement at Southwark on the south bank where features associated with the main road leading northwards to the Thames contained little samian ware and few coins that could be confidently dated earlier than AD 50.

Such a date would seem to preclude a military origin for Londinium, since the legions had long since moved forward by then. Although items of military equipment have been recovered in early levels, they have not appeared in such quantities or concentrations as to represent a legionary base. It had been suggested that one site for a possible fort or camp lay to the west of the city, since part of a large ditch was excavated beneath St Bride's church in 1952, although that feature is now thought to be part of a quarry. A second possibility might lie in the Aldgate area, since V-shaped ditches have been found which look superficially like those which traditionally enclose forts. However, the lengths examined do not join up to form a regular fort, no evidence for any associated barrack blocks has been found (tents would have been used in a Conquest period camp anyway) while ditches with a similar profile have also been noted in 1991 running alongside the Roman precursor of civilian Cheapside. Perhaps such ditches are better seen as evidence of livestock enclosures or similar compounds in this particular phase of development. To sum up, after 20 years of intensive and extensive excavation in the City and Southwark, conclusive evidence of a major military base beneath Londinium has not presented itself: nor have unequivocal traces of even a marching camp been found. The early Roman military site guarding the approach to the Thames, which military logic presumably demands, must be sought elsewhere: sites ranging from the Elephant and Castle to Hyde Park have been suggested.

Town plan

An impression of the extent of the town at this time has also been gained by plotting the distribution of the contemporary cemetery sites, for Roman law decreed that such amenities had to be placed outside the urban settlement zone, and often developed alongside the main roads leading to and from the town. Given that due heed was paid to such laws (which was not always the case), then it follows that the area enclosed by a line drawn through the early Roman cemeteries should define the limits of contemporary London. On the Leadenhall

43

21 *Iron Age round house in Roman London from the Newgate Street site. The 5 x 100mm scale rests on the burnt internal floor of a building destroyed in the Boudican revolt of AD 61. The rest of the building has been cut away by later pits and a large concrete foundation (see also fig.* **22***)* (Museum of London).

Court site for example, which lies close to the highest point of Cornhill, an early Roman quarry had been partially infilled and subsequently used as part of a small cemetery. At least five pottery vessels were found, of which one was still *in situ*, set vertically in the ground, and containing burnt bone. It was a shallow-necked jar in a micaceous sand-tempered fabric, of a type known from other sites in London, dating to the late AD 50s. The neck and rim had been broken off, but the other pots had been even more thoroughly disturbed. Taken together, it seems that a small cemetery had been established here in the mid-first century, and that it had subsequently been sleighted. This presumably took place after the Boudican Revolt, since such an irreverent abuse of a cemetery within a decade of its foundation surely suggests that the despoilers, be they rebels, later settlers or farmers, were not related to those commemorated. What is certain is that, by the AD 60s, the core of Londinium had not expanded that far north. Similar cemeteries have been identified to the east at Billiter Street and to the west near St Paul's, Warwick Square and St Martin-le-Grand,

and these can be taken as indicating the approximate limits of an irregularly-shaped settlement.

When viewed alongside the settlement evidence, the picture of the town becomes clear, as two recent studies have shown. It was based on the eastern hill, in the centre of which an open gravelled area was recorded beneath the site of the later forum near Fenchurch Street and Gracechurch Street: this may represent part of the first unenclosed market place. Settlement seems to have covered a considerable proportion of a wide area focused around Gracechurch Street from the Walbrook to the Lorteburn, where there is evidence for two more east-west roads forming a grid of parallel streets at *c.* 120m intervals. At least two north-south streets have also been identified, of which the one excavated at Whittington Avenue in 1990 can be dated to this period with some confidence. However, the settlement also straggled over the area bisected by the main road leading westwards beyond the Walbrook valley to Newgate (**colour plate 1**), with a similar ribbon development along the Colchester road to Aldgate. There was also some contemporary settlement on the south bank of the Thames, although the full extent of that development has yet to be established. All in all, it seems that the first London incorporated a central core of some 15ha (37 acres) extending over an area of 500m x 300m on the eastern hill, but growing fast. By contrast, the contemporary capital at Camulodunum was already a much grander affair of some 37.5ha (93 acres).

In AD 60, London boasted no prominent public buildings, no masonry villas with mosaic floors as would grace the later Roman city. However, remains of an enigmatic masonry building were found in 1939 on the Allhallows church site in Lombard Street, and another in 1992 beneath the Roman precursor of Bow Lane: such structures are rare in this period and invite speculative interpretation. In the main, the earliest houses seem to have been single storey, timber or brickearth structures with modest-sized rooms. Most of these were rectangular in plan, although some of the buildings recorded on the GPO site in Newgate Street were round-houses (**colour plate 2**), built in the old native style from wattle and daub (**21, 22**). Other examples are now known from London, such as the 4m (13ft) diameter building from 72 Cheapside and the fragment of a 'subcircular' building identified at 86 Fenchurch Street. This suggests something of the racial mix in this settlement, although it is worth noting that one of those buildings was found to contain an imported samian ware platter in its destruction levels: the structure may have been built by natives, but they seemed intent on acquiring the trappings of Romanisation. Examination of the building materials from 35 of the brickearth-walled structures which date to this earliest phase of London's development has identified only three which showed signs of higher-status plaster decoration. All these lay on

22 *Romano-British or Brito-Roman? These plans of mid-first-century buildings are a mixture of native round houses and Roman rectangular structures, all of which were destroyed in AD 61. They were recorded on a site in Newgate Street now occupied by British Telecom (see also fig. 21) (Chrissie Milne).*

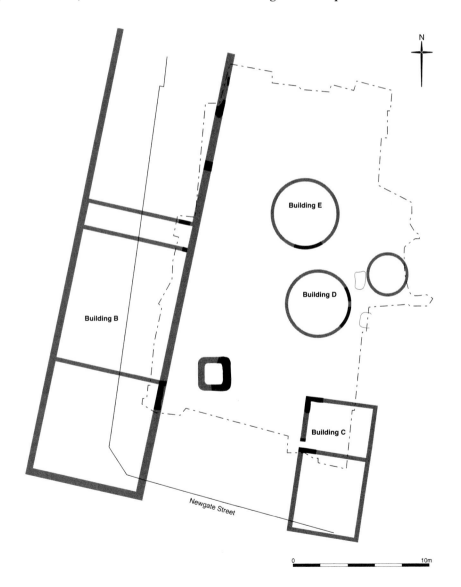

45

the eastern hill, which supports the suggestion that that area comprised the core of the first settlement. Study of the distribution of early Roman pottery from London, whether associated with primary features or disturbed in residual contexts, bears this out. The most significant wares include those from Lyons, from Eccles in Kent, Sugar Loaf Court in London and a particular type of grog and sand-tempered ware, as well as the better-known samian forms such as Ritterling 8 and 9 and Dragendorff 24/25. Finds of this pottery are concentrated in an area extending from the waterfront near London Bridge to just below the crest of the eastern hill, and bordering the road from Newgate to Aldgate.

Trade and industry

Evidence of contemporary industry has also been recovered including glass-blowing debris from the Gateway House site near Watling Court and gem-cutting in Cheapside, where a group of one onyx and three nicolo intaglios were recovered, one of which was unfinished. The Boudican fire levels on the site at 72 Cheapside produced large quantities of charred barley and both emmer and spelt wheat, as well as fragments of quern stone, suggesting the presence of a mill. The burnt cereal recovered from a building in Fenchurch Street is thought to have been imported from the Mediterranean or the Near East, since the deposit contained the non-native Einkorn, lentils and bitter vetch. Although no contemporary harbour facilities have been found, study of the ceramic material shows that substantial cargoes of imported material like fine pottery, olive oil and wine were arriving in London at this date.

Further evidence of contemporary industries has been gained from study of the areas on the periphery of the settlement. For example, deposits of London Clay, sands and gravels were exposed on the foreshore near Billingsgate, and the earliest Roman activity included quarry pits up to 11m (36ft) across, presumably dug to extract this material. Other features recorded on the river bank near Fish Street Hill include part of an early Roman building associated with a timber-lined tank set in a wide clay-lined pit. This may have been part of a fish-processing complex examined in more detail in later levels on the neighbouring site. More evidence of the industrial rather than commercial use of the river bank was recorded on the Sugar Loaf Court site, to the west of the Walbrook stream near Huggin Hill. Early Roman buildings were recorded, together with burnt clay which probably came from the lining of a kiln and fragments of waste vessels, the fabric of which was of a hitherto unknown type. This seems to represent a pottery manufacturing site, presumably set outside the contemporary settlement, but located so as to take advantage of the London Clay exposed on the foreshore at low tide. The products of this kiln have been recovered from levels associated with the Boudican revolt or from earlier phases, but it seems that the potter (perhaps an immigrant from Gaul) perished in the uprising or moved elsewhere, since his pottery has not been identified in significant quantities in later levels. Among the more remarkable products was a wine amphora, suggesting that native vineyards were already in commercial production by this date. In sum, the Thames foreshore saw considerable and varied activity in the early decades of Roman occupation, but it was of an appreciably different character from that which followed.

The founding of Londinium

In the oft-quoted description this phase of the settlement taken from Tacitus' *Annals* (see Chapter 1), the settlement does not seem to have been awarded official legal recognition as a fully-fledged *municipium* at this stage. This could imply that it was a planned town but, since construction work was still underway, the status which would be conferred upon it was being delayed until the appropriate moment. After all, it had as yet, no public buildings to speak of. Alternatively, it might be regarded as a settlement which developed almost organically, serving a crucial trans-shipment function that had not been wholly foreseen. However, it is possible to argue that the impetus for this urban development does seem to have enjoyed a measure of official support, since evidence of a central plan can be identified. Houses were laid out within property boundaries which were often (but not always) sufficiently defined to re-emerge on the same lines after the disaster of AD 61; a regular plan has been traced in the lines of contemporary metalled streets, which were well-made and provided with road-side ditches. From such evidence as has been recovered, it is suggested that at least the bare framework of the settlement on the eastern hill conformed to an Imperial idea, rather than growing completely haphazardly like a gold-rush town. Nevertheless, the settlement was not a model new town: although it may well have been sanctioned, its growth was neither closely nor rigorously controlled. That it was rapidly expanding seems clear: in AD 60 London was busy rather than beautiful, a bustling if unembellished T-shaped town (**23**, and see **20**).

Study of the finds evidence now suggests that the first London grew up sometime after AD 50, that is, it developed only after the military had moved forward to Wales and the north, in what was then regarded as the pacified hinterland set safely behind the front line. Its does not seem to have been founded until after the road system had been re-aligned in this area and the new Thames crossing established, some seven years or so after the initial invasion. Since the roads were laid out under the orders of the new administration, the settlement presumably won at least the blessing of the Governor, and need not be seen as a spontaneous development of merchant entrepreneurs. Nevertheless, the scale

23 *Remains of timber buildings dating to the birth of Londinium in AD 50–60 were recorded in this shaft dug for the Docklands Light Railway in Bucklersbury in 1987* (Museum of London).

of its subsequent growth was probably not foreseen, since it outgrew its rudimentary grid within a decade. Indeed, Dominic Perring's recent study of Roman London was able to identify two clear phases of marked expansion within this short period.

By AD 60 then, the Romans were confident of their mastery of the south-eastern corner of the newly-won province, so confident that substantial defences for Londinium were deemed unnecessary. Not for the first time, the Romans demonstrated a costly inability to understand the province or to predict the future course of events. Whatever London lacked in official status seemed of no concern to Boudica's army of liberation: alongside its more distinguished neighbours of Verulamium and Camulodunum, it was clearly significant enough to merit sacking. Within a decade of its foundation, Londinium was totally destroyed.

5

New town

The Boudican Revolt was duly suppressed by the Roman military machine and the 25 years which followed it saw the town transformed from a modest but precocious settlement to one of some stature. For the burnt-out remains of Londinium in AD 61, however, recovery was not a foregone conclusion. The province was shaken, there was widespread famine, a crisis of confidence, financial restrictions. The rebuilding of many of the burnt properties in London was slow, suggesting that survivors were few. There were some exceptions to that rule: dendrochronological studies of timber from a site in Cheapside excavated in 1990 show that the rebuilding there incorporated timbers felled in AD 62, and evidence from a site in Eastcheap suggests immediate redevelopment with the new building (B4) raised directly over the site of the old. Many other properties show little sign of major activity until about AD 70, when the settlement finally took off again: by then rebuilding on the old lines had taken place on sites in Fenchurch Street, Birchin Lane and St Swithins Lane on the eastern side of town for example, while new roads accompanied the redevelopments at Well Court and Ironmonger Lane in the west. Over the Thames in Southwark, the road-building programme was extended, associated with mudbrick and timber buildings on some sites, although there was also new masonry building incorporating timbers felled in AD 73–4. However, there was a full 30 year delay before some sites, such as one in Lime Street on the

north bank, were rebuilt. Whatever the final date for reconstruction, it is significant how often the pre AD 60 alignments and boundaries re-emerged in the new layouts on some sites, even though the old building lines had been masked by debris or otherwise obliterated. This seems to suggest that some sort of landholding register may have been kept, and that properties before and after the fire were entered in it.

This is not to say that the new town was a duplicate of the old, for it was not. Work began on a wide range of public facilities, often associated with road building schemes: once the trauma of the revolt had been overcome, redevelopment began in earnest.

Recovery

Before the range of new public works is described, it would be instructive to look in detail at one particular site to consider the stages through which the town slowly recovered. Our example is the Leadenhall Court/ Whittington Avenue site examined between 1985 and 1989, on the crest of Cornhill next to a north–south road (24). Initially, it seems that this area lay close to the northern limit of the mid-first-century settlement, marked by a small cemetery and an east–west ditch and post-built fence. That alignment is traceable in the topography of the area for the next half-century suggesting that that particular boundary may represent one of the major land subdivisions of the early settlement: it may even represent the northern boundary of

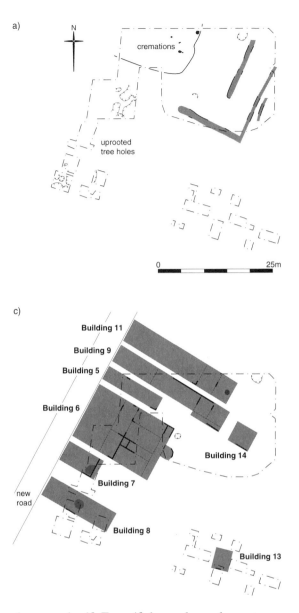

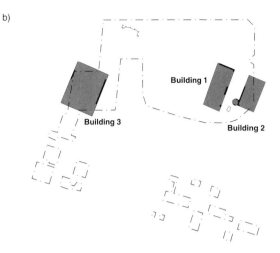

24 *Urban Growth. The Leadenhall Court site lay just outside the first Roman settlement in AD 60 (a), as the presence of a cremation cemetery shows. After the Boudican uprising, subsistence farming was the order of the day (b), represented by these widely-spaced farm buildings. By AD 75 (c) the settlement was transformed with the introduction of closely spaced urban housing laid fronting a new street to the west* (Chrissie Milne).

the town itself. Even if the early settlement were not blessed with military defences, its boundaries may well have been clearly defined. After the revolt in AD 61 signs that the settlement was encroaching become apparent, as the area was comprehensively deturfed and levelled. Although a series of irregular tree-holes was recorded in one area, the artificial horizon thus created was generally free of major root disturbance. This action provided a stable, level building platform, a supply of Brickearth for building material, a quantity of turves, topsoil, and a stockpile of

wood and timber from the uprooted trees. It also represents an unequivocally determined act of redevelopment, a clear demonstration of future intent. Samples from the tree-hole fills suggest that the area at the time was dominated by grassland and arable weeds, including hay, suggesting several different farming-related activities.

An extensive slab of brickearth was then spread over much of the site, to prepare the ground for new buildings, of which two were recorded on the east side of the site. Examination of material derived from a third building, set to the south, shows that, in contrast to the other contemporary structures, its walls had been embellished with painted wall plaster and it may have had a tiled roof. This building therefore stands out as the principal building in this first group. Quantities of domestic refuse were dumped over the disused cemetery, presumably by the occupants of newly erected buildings. An associated midden was particularly rich in wetland species and also contained mainly waste land plants and arable weeds such as field penny-cress, sheep's sorrel, and hairy buttercup, while another sample contained plants likely to have grown in a farm yard.

Shortly after Building 1 was demolished, a quarry some 5m ($16\frac{1}{2}$ft) in diameter was dug to extract Brickearth, presumably for another new building, which was aligned east–west. Both this and the preceding phase produced the usual mix of seeds found on Roman urban sites, with weeds of waste and disturbed ground pre-dominating. However, wasteland and arable weeds were common in a sample from an external dump associated with the later phase as was a significantly high number of grassland seeds including buttercups, lesser stitchwort, cinquefoil/tormentil, parsley piert and wild carrot. The rural nature of the site in this period was underlined by study of the animal bones. This identified examples of new born calves, lambs and piglets amongst the material recovered from this phase. Bones from such creatures (neonates) are unlikely to have been moved over

large distances, which suggests that stock rearing was taking place in the immediate vicinity. Interestingly, neonates have only been identified on two other sites of this period, one just to the north in Bishopsgate, the other to the south at Eastcheap. The interpretation of these Leaden-hall Court buildings as working farms or small holdings is further supported by the presence of a larger quantity of bones from horse, dog and goose in this phase, as well as by the discovery of some cart fittings.

It is noteworthy that the building development was focused on the east side of the site, and that evidence of horticultural activity next to a main road was recorded on the Whittington Avenue site to the east, where the buildings destroyed by fire were not replaced. Instead the area was turned over to cultivation, since narrow, linear grooves each up to 500mm (20in.) in length were recorded on the underlying surface. There was no strict pattern to the grooves, suggesting more than one season's cultivation. Micromorpho-logical examination showed that the grooves were lined with a manure-like deposit, demon-strating that the allotment had been comprehen-sively composted before planting. It is therefore suggested that the cluster of buildings which include Building 3 represent a widely-spaced development surrounded by fields or allotments, set back from that main road leading north from the more densely occupied centre of the early Roman settlement. The disposition of the build-ings around a yard, together with the botanical and faunal evidence, combine to suggest that this part of Londinium contained farms: self-sufficiency was the order of the day, as the province tried to rebuild itself in the aftermath of the Boudican uprising.

This part of the town was comprehensively re-planned in AD 75 following the construction of the new forum to the south, and its associated roads and fresh *insulae*. A more formal layout was established with closely-spaced houses set out over the area (**25**), to the rear of which were single-roomed outhouses, wells, latrine pits and middens. Although it was partially based on

25 *Remains of a first-century building on the Leaden-hall Court site, cut by later pits and steel girders. The 10 x 100mm scale rests on the brickearth floor of a modest mud-walled building: traces of its narrow walls can be seen. An alley 1m (3ft) wide – cut by the oval medieval pit – separates this property from the one to the south (top of photo)* (Museum of London).

a)

b)

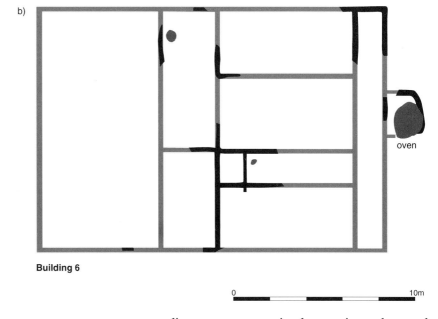

oven

Building 6

0   10m

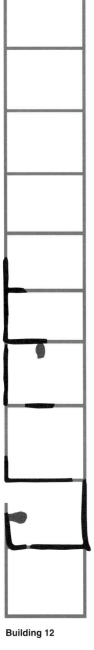

Building 12

26 *Town houses in the late first century on the Leadenhall Court site: a) lower class: shops and workshops on street frontage (top) with cheap rented accommodation to the rear (Building 12); b) middle class: residential building with kitchen at back (Building 6) (Chrissie Milne).*

alignments set out in the previous phases, the focus of this new plan now faced west, with the new frontage laid out along the principal north-south road which lay beneath modern Grace-church street. Of the new buildings examined on the Leadenhall Court site, Building 6 seems to have been the largest and to have lasted the longest. Its walls were founded on squared timber base-plates and enclosed several inter-connecting rooms: at least some of the rooms were adorned with painted wall plaster and the roof may have been tiled. It is perhaps significant that it directly replaced Building 3, another structure of higher quality than its immediate neighbours. It is suggested that the owner of Building 3 may have been one of the more successful new inhabitants of this part of the town, prospering sufficiently to build the larger Buil-ding 6. It is also possible to argue that the owner of that structure may also have owned part of the new insula, while some of the inferior quality buildings clustered around it may have been occupied by tenants.

In marked contrast to Building 6 (**26**), the other structures were strip buildings comprising a simpler arrangement of square rooms aligned one behind the other. Access to the rooms was not through the buildings, but via one of the narrow gravel alleyways which ran from the principal thoroughfare in the west to the back-yards in the east. This implies that such structures were designed for more than one family unit: perhaps the main tenant lived and worked in the westernmost rooms, next to the principal thoroughfare, while sub-tenants occupied the rooms to the east. Such a division might account for the way that additional rooms were added to or subtracted from several of these strip buildings during their life, each self-contained unit of one or two rooms being built when new tenants arrived and demolished as they left without unduly affecting the stability of the

27 A new town centre laid out in the late first century. New streets, forum, and temple are shown in relation to a sample from the Leadenhall Court site of dense urban housing characteristic of this period (Chrissie Milne).

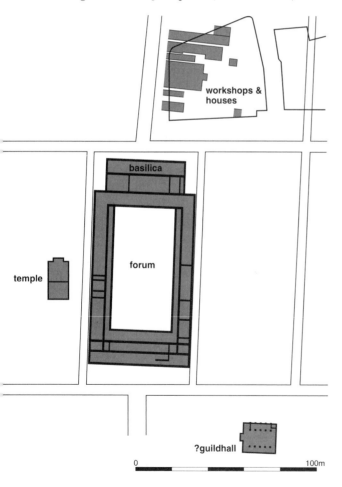

building or the lives of the other families. The distribution of the pottery and finds from all these buildings was examined to see if it reflected the differing status, prosperity and degree of 'Romanisation' of the inhabitants. It has been found, for example, that ceramic beakers in a sandy grey ware and pottery fired by reduction in the native tradition appear more commonly on lower, rather than higher, status sites, while a significant proportion of wine amphorae seems to indicate the more prosperous households. The ceramic assemblage associated with Building 6 supported the suggestion that it was a higher status household compared to its neighbours, as did the building material, which included roof tile and painted wall-plaster. The associated bone assemblage showed a 'Romanised' preference for pig, in contrast to the evidence from the strip buildings where sheep was more common, together with 'low status' items such as the fish known as smelt. By such combined studies of building plans, associated artefacts and environmental evidence, a surprisingly detailed social, commercial and topographical history of the settlement can be compiled.

Town centre

Perhaps the most significant development of all for the new town was the building of its first forum and basilica, forming the new civic centre (**27**). This was laid out over the mid-first-century metalled market area at the head of the road leading downhill to the river crossing. Fragments of the large complex some 100m north–south by 50m east–west have been examined piecemeal over many years. However, their identification as part of a first-century forum was obscured by the remains of a later and larger forum which overlay them. Subsequent work by the DUA clarified the situation. Observations in a tunnel in 1977–8 (**28**) and excavations in Gracechurch Street in 1983–4 refined the plan and dating of the complex, and the results were published in 1987. It comprised four wings arranged around a central courtyard: the basilica lay to the north with a nave separated from the side aisles by

28 Evidence of the first civic centre redevelopment was recorded in this cable trench below Gracechurch Street in 1977 (Museum of London).

columns or piers, and a tribunal at the east end. The east and west wings initially contained a single range of rooms which opened out onto the courtyard, but an inner portico was added subsequently. The south wing had a double range of rooms, of which the outer ones presumably opened out onto the main east–west street. To the east of the forum was a classical temple some 20m (66ft) long by 10m (33ft) wide, set within its own precinct. To the south-east, on the opposite side of the main east-west road below Fenchurch Street, an aisled hall some 18m (59ft) long by 14m (46ft) wide was excavated. It was built with mudbricks over a baseplate laid on deeply-set gravel and mortar footings and its walls were rendered with painted plaster or mortar internally and externally: it may have served as an assembly hall for a town guild. Here then was a complex of buildings which was the embodiment of the Roman ideal of urban life, a place where religion, commerce and administration could meet and mingle.

New public facilities

Other public buildings graced the new town, including two bath-houses, one examined in the 1950s in Cheapside, and a larger complex hurriedly recorded in the 1960s (**29**) and then in more detail in 1988–9. This was built between AD 70–90 at the foot of Huggin Hill, terraced into the steep hillside next to the Thames, but below the spring line which fed the baths. A concrete raft supported by a field of piles formed the base of the building which comprised a suite of heated and unheated rooms on the 4m (13ft) OD terrace laid out parallel to the Thames. The rooms represented included a hot room (*caldarium*) containing a basin for ablutions in the south apse, a warm room (*tepidarium*), a cold room (*frigidarium*), as well as changing rooms and a hot bath in the north near the furnace. A jetty or entrance way may have led into a riverside room on the southern side. The exercise yard (*palaestra*) probably lay to the east while service areas, furnaces and water-tanks were located along the northern side of the complex.

In the north-west of the town a large timber structure was erected of which part of the eastern side was examined on the extensive and spectacular Guildhall site between 1985 and 1994. It incorporated a row of squared posts set in a curving foundation trench, to the west of which was an open yard surface. This has been identified as an amphitheatre in which the earthen bank which formed the seating for the arena was retained by a timber revetment. Provisional dating from samples examined by the dendrochronologist show that timber felled sometime after AD 70 was used in this phase.

Between AD 70 and 80, the line of the embanked Thames waterfront had been extended southwards into the river with the construction of a vast artificial terrace at the foot of the steeply-sloping hillside. It comprised an infill of dumped material retained by a framework of braced timber baulks stacked horizontally one upon the other. It seems to have provided a uniform frontage with a level surface at least 1m (3ft) above high-tide level, and may have

29 *Public building: part of the Huggin Hill bath-house recorded in 1969, looking north-east. The 4 x 1ft imperial scale rests on the floor of heated Room 30* (Museum of London).

extended from Regis House and Miles Lane in the east to the Walbrook in the west: a small extension was recorded in 1979 near St James Garlickhithe on the western bank of the confluence. Although this feature has been described as a quay, it does not necessarily imply that its function was solely commercial and that the town's port facilities, warehouses and berths for shipping extended along its entire length. This particular development may have been as much concerned with providing a flood defence, access (as a road or towpath) and building land at the foot of the very steeply-sloping hillside as with mercantile opportunity. By way of analogy, the Victoria Embankment set out in the 1870s was not a commercial quay but accommodated a road, gardens, an underground railway and a main sewer. However, to the the east of the Miles Lane Roman quay, beyond an inlet at the foot of the road leading down to the river from the forum, a different type of timber waterfront structure was recorded, an openwork landing stage at least 57m (187ft) long. It presumably marked the northern end of the ferry crossing over the Thames. The foreshore beneath it was littered with broken pottery, oyster shells, wood shavings and barrel fragments including non-native softwoods. This suggests that such containers were being broken up on the waterfront in this area. To the east of the landing stage the bank was retained by more modest post and plank revetments. No trace of a bridge which functioned with any of these structures has yet been found: it is just possible therefore that Londinium was still relying on ferries to provide the link to the southern shore (see **30**).

A town established

It seems reasonable to suppose that Londinium was now distinguished with a new urban authority and enjoyed a new role in the province. It was provided with a range of public facilities, streets and harbour works: the *insulae* were filling up with buildings (**30**). Development was not confined to the heart of the town in the vicinity of the forum. New roads laid out at this date have been recorded in 1979 near Bow Lane, where a north-south street was established at the same time as new buildings. A similar pattern was observed at Ironmonger Lane in 1980 where an east-west street was laid out for the first time in *c.* AD 70. At the other side of town near Aldgate the line of the earlier road was not respected by the new developments, for two new streets were set out, against which new buildings were constructed. Public buildings have also been provisionally identified in Southwark, on the opposite bank of the Thames. For example, the well-appointed masonry building constructed in *c.* AD 74, with a courtyard 20m (66ft) across, may be a public lodging or inn, a *mansio*. But above all it is the construction of the forum on the north bank which sums up the new town:

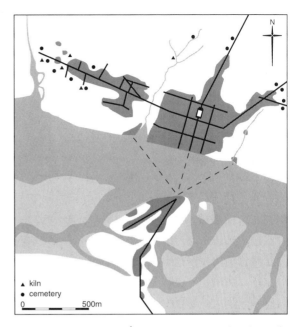

30 *London in AD 80. This plan shows a notable phase of expansion after the Boudican revolt; cf., fig. **20**. Dashed lines indicate possible ferry routes* (Chrissie Milne).

here was an expression of faith on behalf of the authorities of the comfortable but businesslike future it had planned for Londinium.

6

Capital city

The paint was hardly dry on the new town when the builders moved in again. In a quite extraordinary fervour, Londinium was upgraded and replanned and by the turn of the century it was reborn as the provincial capital. New streets were laid out, the Walbrook valley was infilled, the port facilities extended, public buildings enlarged, a fort for the Governor's bodyguard built (or rebuilt). This was not gradual growth but a sudden explosion, and it is nowhere better exemplified than in the heart of the town, its civic centre, the forum and basilica. Development of the civic centre in Londinium had began in *c.* AD 70, with the building of the comparatively modest forum described in Chapter 5, but now more ambitious plans were laid, symbols of a new order. These required the clearance of a large area of the contemporary town centre, including that already occupied by the earlier forum (**31**). The new structure was to be 170m wide and 170m long, nearly four times the size of its predecessor (**colour plate 9**). The town clearly intended to expand in a big way.

The initial construction process took up to 30 years to complete, a fact which reflects both the complexity of the forum project and the level of resources which it required. On the northern side was the basilica. This was not built in one phase, but had a complex development: neither of the aisles was part of the primary scheme, for example. The recent work has shown that there was only one apse, at the eastern end of the long nave which ran almost the whole length of the new building: in addition there was a portico beyond the apse at the eastern end. There was a single range of offices on the northern side of the nave (**32**), but access beyond them to the most northerly rooms could only be gained from the street to the north. These are now inter-preted as shops, separated from each other by temporary partition walls. To the south, the second-century forum consisted of three wings enclosing a rectangular courtyard, some 100m east–west and 85m north–south, the evidence coming from thirteen sites investigated from 1881 to 1977. In the first phase, the east and west wings incorporated three ranges of rooms comprising two sets of shops or offices with an external portico, but an inner portico facing the courtyard was subsequently added. These two wings may have been joined in the middle by a colonnaded walkway which spanned the central courtyard. The south wing seems to have comprised a single range of rooms with internal and external porticos and a major monumental entrance.

The fate of houses which were cleared away for the new scheme has also been studied. Shortly after AD 85, rooms fell into disuse and were gradually demolished as the population was moved out. The buildings in the north of the site were then converted into site huts for the construction workers. Work began on the new basilica with the digging of deep foundation trenches. The evidence from the Leadenhall Court site was sufficiently detailed to identify many features of the building site, including the

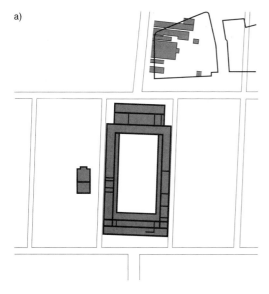

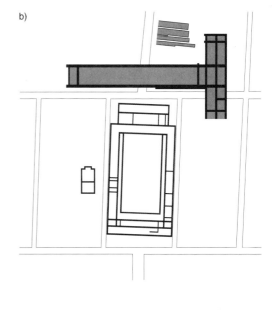

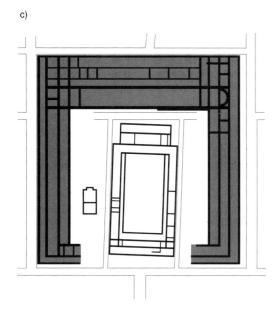

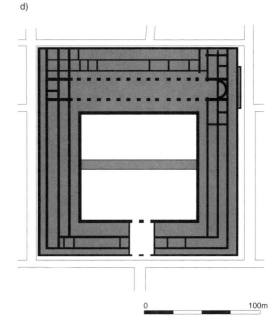

0   100m

31 *Civic centre redevelopment: between AD 85 and 140 the heart of the city was transformed. The modest but functional forum (a) was retained for twenty years while a much larger complex was gradually built up around it (b, c). By the mid second century, Londinium had the largest forum and basilica in the province (d) (Chrissie Milne).*

workers' huts and stores, mortar mixing pits and even the hoof prints of the pack animals which brought the ragstone rubble from the waterfront at the foot of the hill. The basilica itself was built initially in two phases, and it is suggested that the east and west wings of the forum were constructed at the same time as, or shortly after that second phase. The outer walls of the wings continued north to form the outer porticos of the basilica. It seems that the first-century civic centre probably remained standing for some time, since internal colonnades were added to its south wing and inward-facing aisles during this period. Clearly the city felt it could no longer function without its forum, and a complicated building programme was devised to ensure the smooth running of the town during the transi-

32 *The 10 x 100mm scale lies next to a fragment of the second-century basilica wall and foundation exposed on the Leadenhall Court site in 1986. Although damaged by later action, the scale of the complex can be appreciated from the size of this one room in the northern range* (Museum of London).

tional period. Only after the new basilica was brought into operation could the first forum be demolished. Then the new south wing was built and an inner portico added, connected to the south side of the basilica. Significant variation was apparent in the details of construction and dimension in several sections of the same primary forum wall, suggesting that the project was built in stages over an extended period. The construction of this much enlarged complex necessitated the laying out of new roads around

the forum and basilica, which attracted new buildings, workshops and commercial premises to fill the insulae thus created (**colour plate 7**).

The Provincial Governor

It seems clear that London's role was expanding in this period, which must imply increased imperial interest. The construction of the fort at Cripplegate to the north and west of the main centre of population but conveniently next to the amphitheatre is an unambiguous sign of this, since the fort presumably housed the 1000-strong contingent of troops seconded from the legions to serve the provincial governor (**33**). It was some 200m north–south by 200m east–west with masonry walls supported by towers at the four gates and the four corners as well as at intervals between them. Traces of at least three barrack

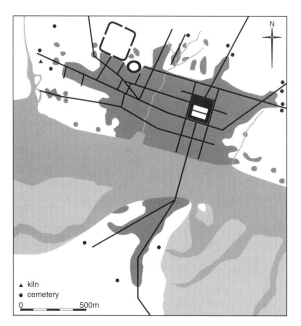

33 *Plan of London in the early second century. The town has expanded dramatically; cf., fig.* **30** *(Chrissie Milne).*

blocks have been recorded in the interior, and sections cut across the V-shaped ditch which ran round the exterior of the fort. The majority of the work on this major feature was conducted by Professor Grimes starting in the late 1940s, with the Guildhall Museum extending the research in the 1960s. Work in the late 1980s has added little to the picture, since the recent sites proved to be badly truncated and very disturbed. However, work at the site at 55 Basing-hall Street located the fort ditch in 1989, with traces of a timber structure just to the west. The wall itself had been robbed but the backfilled ditch was sealed by floors and walls of later Roman buildings.

It would seem that the fort with its stone walls was laid out between AD 90 and 120, although the question of an earlier timber defensive circuit is still unresolved. The recent discovery of the neighbouring timber amphitheatre dated to the 70s and of a contemporary road apparently leading to the southern gate of the fort has re-opened this important discussion.

New public facilities

The forum-basilica was not the only building to have been substantially enlarged by the early second century. The main public baths at Huggin Hill (**34**) were extensively rebuilt with the addition of another large hot room (*caldarium*) to the north. Parts of the original complex had to be pulled down to accommodate this. The under-floor heating system was redesigned, as was the drainage system, with the insertion of new timber-lined drains. Likewise, the Cheapside baths were extensively modified at the same time. New floors and a hypocaust were added in some rooms, while the northern room was rebuilt to allow for the insertion of a new furnace.

The amphitheatre was also completely rebuilt, this time with walls with ragstone rubble foundations over which tile footings were laid. The entrance way was flanked by small chambers with stone-flagged thresholds leading into the arena which, it has been calculated,

34 *Work progresses on the underfloor heating system of the Huggin Hill bath-house in 1989. A survey is being made of the tile stacks* (pilae) *in this large public building* (Museum of London).

35 *Guildhall Yard, the church of St Lawrence to the left, Guildhall to the right. The Yard itself is laid out over the arena of the Roman amphitheatre, some wall fragments of which can just be seen curving beneath the rectilinear brick walls crossing the excavation in the foreground. The two 10 x 100mm scales rest on the arena, to either side of the timber-lined drain* (Museum of London).

formed an oval area some 100m wide at its maximum extent. It was crossed by a well-preserved timber drain, a necessary feature in this area which, although set high on the western hill, is close to a tributary of the Walbrook. The fill of this drain contained five human skull fragments as well as leg and jaw bones, together with the skull of a bull: an evocative if grisly assemblage (**35, 36**).

Industrial quarter

To say that the settlement was also extended north-west of the new forum in this period is correct, but does not do justice to the work involved. This area incorporated part of the head waters of the Walbrook, which, at the beginning of the Roman period, was a clean and slow flowing stream meandering through a marshy landscape. There were at least four channels, each one between 20m and 50m wide, which carried tributaries of the Walbrook to the confluence just north of the Bank of England, beneath Kings Arms Yard. Each of these valleys contained a body of running water between 3m and 9m wide. The main channel itself was up to 100m across and 10m deep. This river system with its defiles presented a challenge to the Roman town planners, since it effectively divided the town in two. The answer to the problem was a typically Roman response: they decided to fill the valley in, thereby removing an unsightly topographical constraint. Each channel was subsequently infilled with dumps of clay and gravel while the streams were canalised between timber revetments. It was a substantial if not

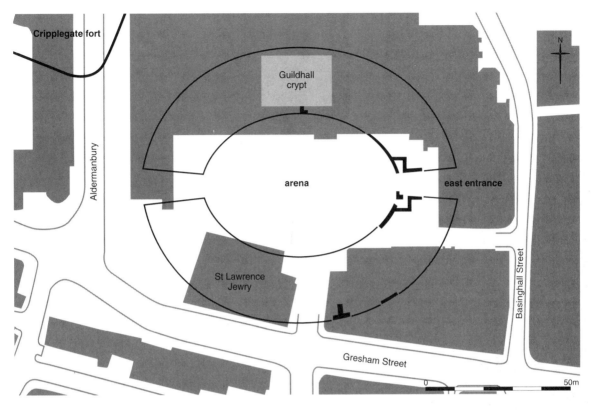

36 *The outline of the London amphitheatre shown in relation to the medieval crypt beneath Guildhall, the church of St Lawrence Jewry, and the curves in the alignment of present-day Basinghall Street and Gresham Street. The presence of his large Roman feature seems to have exercised a substantial influence on the subsequent development of this part of the City* (Chrissie Milne).

wholly successful undertaking, as recent studies graphically show. Nevertheless, some twenty years later, the unsightly dissected plateau had been levelled up and the area had been sufficiently cut by drainage channels to allow occupation to begin (**colour plate 3**).

After several false starts, a substantial road 6m (20ft) wide was eventually raised over a raft of branches and a stack of turf, high enough to avoid the consequences of flooding in this waterlogged area. A second road was laid out parallel to it to the east, and timber buildings were erected along them (**37, 38**). These seem to have functioned both as domestic residences and work-shops, to judge by the artefacts recovered

from the associated levels. Evidence of a variety of industries has been recovered from the Walbrook area, suggesting that there was a particular concentration of such activities in this zone. Pottery seems to have been manufactured in the area between Copthall Close and the Bank of England since wasters and debris have been found there. The distinctive black pottery with compass-drawn decoration known as 'London ware' and mica-dusted wares seem to have been made here between AD 90-130, suggesting that a ready source of good clay and a plentiful supply of firewood were to hand. Debris from a smithy was recovered from the middle Walbrook valley, in the form of much slag and a large assemblage of 2456 used nails, ripe for recycling. Again, this suggests a ready supply of firewood nearby. From Copthall Avenue there was bone-working, to produce such items as weaving tablets. But perhaps the most commonly represented was leather-working: waste from this industry was recovered from many Walbrook sites, and was present throughout the occupation sequence. It

37 *Timber base-plate of a building from the Copthall Avenue site, preserved in the waterlogged conditions of the Walbrook valley (5 x 100mm scale)* (Museum of London).

38 *Excavating a brickearth wall of a Roman building on the London Wall site. It was constructed during the redevelopment of the upper Walbrook valley* (Museum of London).

may well reflect one of the town's principal products in this period (**39**). The 52 London Wall excavation, for example, produced one of the largest collections of shoe-making waste from any City site, and included men's, women's and children's footwear, hob-nailed shoes, sandals and one-piece moccasins. Another vast dump of leather shoes was recovered from Dowgate Hill House in 1987 in the mouth of the Walbrook, but that was late third-century in date. Evidence of tanning has been found in the area, while Professor Grimes recorded an animal hide still pegged out on the St Swithin's House site. The leather industry may have been associated in

39 *Hob-nail boots. Nail patterns on a selection of leather soles discarded on a late first- to early second-century waterfront site near Billingsgate in 1974* (Sue Hurman after David Parfitt).

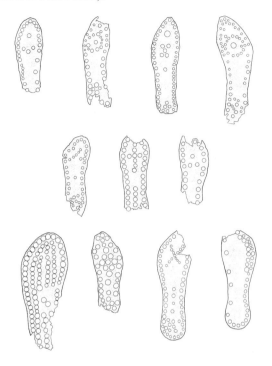

part with a contract for military supplies: the Cripplegate fort lay but a short distance to the west for example.

In addition to ample evidence of more leather-working, the 55 Moorgate site was one of a number which produced glass-working debris, phials, cups, jars, and jewellery, as well as part of a tank furnace, all associated with an early second-century brickearth and timber building (**40**). Appropriately enough, a stone statue of Mercury was also found, suggesting that there was a shrine to the god of commerce in the vicinity (**colour plate 4**). In 1993, excavations on the western side of the Walbrook valley at Guildhall Yard produced the largest collection of cullet, that is glass collected for recycling, from any Romano-British town. It is worth stressing that the workshops associated with these industries were modest in size and were distributed

40 *Industrial zone. Many small workshops engaged in leather and glass-working were established in the Walbrook valley in the second century. These examples were recorded near Moorgate in 1987* (Chrissie Milne).

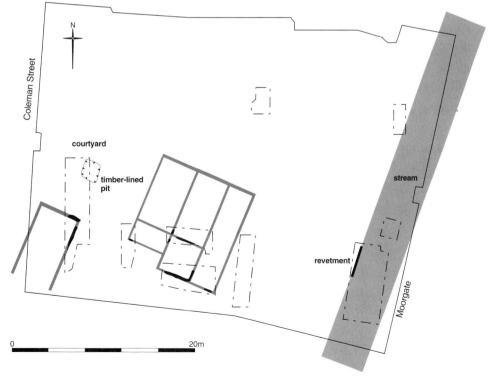

over a wide area. The work seems to have been conducted on a family basis, rather than in centrally-organised factory units.

At the mouth of the Walbrook, the wide confluence with the Thames was radically altered. Both sides of the valley were revetted and two separate channels, divided by an artificial island, now brought the water down into the Thames. Perhaps the best explanation for such a major change in the regime of the river is that a watermill (or indeed a series of mills) had been set up. One possible location has already been suggested on the Bucklersbury House site, where three mill stones were found. Two were lower stones, the other an upper stone with the notch for the drive shaft. Burnt grain and carbonised wheat were recorded on the National Safe Deposit site nearby, perhaps the store for the mill. The discovery in 1990 of another complete millstone on the Pinner Hall site in Old Broad Street suggests that a second mill may have been built higher up the valley. A similar situation was recorded in 1990 on the western side of the city. Drainage of an island in the Fleet River was carried out in the late first century, after which a building associated with wheat chaff (interpreted as a mill), a jetty and a warehouse were erected after AD 116, according to the dendrochronological report. They continued in use until the end of the century. Taken together, it now seems that there is clear evidence for a deliberate development of water engineering and for water-powered mill construction as well as donkey-mills in London in this period.

London's bridge

Changes were also taking place down on the waterfront, where the first clear evidence for

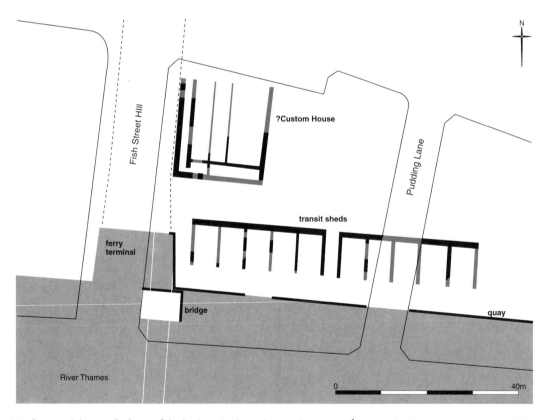

41 *Commercial zone: the heart of the harbour in the early second century. The quay, bridge pier and storage buildings were recorded in 1979–82 on sites in Pudding Lane. The building on the higher terrace to the north which may have functioned as an administrative office for the port was excavated on the Fish Street Hill site in 1985* (Chrissie Milne).

1 *Londinium in AD 60, before the Boudican uprising. The view is along the street later known as Newgate Street, looking north-west. Shops front the main road with native-style round houses in the back yards* (reconstruction by John Pearson).

2 *The 5x100mm scale is sited on the beaten earth floor of a second-century building found on the Newgate Street site. A major fire destroyed most of this mud-brick and timber building, leaving the stubs of its walls, burnt pottery from a kitchen cupboard and the remains of a brick hearth* (Museum of London).

3 *Londinium in the second century: light industry and commercial premises expand over the newly-reclaimed land in the Walbrook valley. A reconstruction by John Pearson, based on the excavations at Copthall Avenue and neighbouring sites.*

4 *This statue of Mercury, god of commerce, was discovered on a Moorgate excavation in 1987 (Museum of London).*

5 *The heart of the harbour in early second-century London, looking towards the first bridge over the Thames, and showing the warehouses and timber-faced quays. This model is based on the results of a series of excavations near Billingsgate between 1979 and 1982 (Museum of London).*

6 *Excavations in progress in 1981 on the Roman quay near Pudding Lane. The early second-century warehouse just to the north of the timber quay is being cleaned up for photography (Museum of London).*

7 *A bakehouse in Roman London, with its large bread ovens. On the far side of the street outside is the forum – the civic centre. This reconstruction by Martin Bentley is based on excavations at Birchin Lane, which lay on the western side of the forum.*

8 *The excavation of a second-century tavern in Fenchurch Street in 1983 produced fragments of wall plaster which represented a robed human figure (Museum of London).*

9 *Part of the great Basilica was uncovered during the excavations at Leadenhall Court in 1985-6. The foundations seen here were part of the north-east corner of a building the size of St Paul's Cathedral (Museum of London).*

10 *The traffic and trade of the Roman town can be traced through studies of pottery recovered from excavations within the ancient town. A range of imported pottery is shown here, together with a clay figurine (Museum of London).*

11 *Recent research has suggested that work on a palace complex began in AD 293 in the area close to St Peter's Hill off Upper Thames Street. This reconstruction by Peter Froste shows construction underway on that prestigious building.*

12 *This mosaic pavement graced a building with mud-brick walls found in Milk Street in 1976. It was sealed beneath dark grey silt deposits which marked the end of Roman occupation on this site* (Museum of London).

42 *Recording the timber-floored warehouse on the Pudding Lane site* (Museum of London).

London's bridge, a new quay, a set of warehouses and a possible custom house had all been built as part of the same development by the early second century (**41** and **colour plate 5**). The bridge pier was set on the foreshore to the south of the inlet at the foot of what is now Fish Street Hill. It was made, not of stone, but of timber, comprising a timber box some 7m by 5m (23 x 16ft), still standing over 2m (6½ft) tall. It is thought to have been one of several piers which supported the decking for the bridge itself (see Chapter 10). Some 160m to the south of this point a concentration of coins was found in the Thames between 1824 and 1841 during dredging: they were collected and published by Charles Roach-Smith, who recognised that the

finds spot marked the position of the old bridge. The coins are thought to have been votive offerings thrown into the Thames from a shrine on the bridge: this may have had an altar to Neptune, since a lead curse to Neptune (*Metunus*) was discovered on the foreshore nearby in 1984. The Roman bridge at Newcastle had a similar shrine, for altars to Neptune and Oceanus were found there. If the London shrine was built in the middle of the bridge, then that structure would have been over 320m long. A recent study of the coins found in the nineteenth-century has shown that there were far more coins of the date AD 70–81 then in the earlier or later issues, from which it is suggested that the bridge was built sometime after AD 70–81, i.e., not in AD 50: dendrochronological and stratigraphic analysis had previously suggested a date of between AD 85 and 90 for its construction.

Commercial quarter

The openwork landing stage which lay just north of the bridge had been partially dismantled and replaced by an infilled quay (**colour plate 6**) of the type previously seen at Miles Lane to the east. The timbers of the south-west corner of the new quay had been partially cut through the ends of those of the bridge pier, although it is clear that both bridge and quay must have functioned together ultimately. The two ranges of open-fronted, five-bay buildings which were erected over the newly won land are seen as transit sheds or warehouses (**42**).

An integral part of this development, which included the provision of drains designed to disgorge into the Thames through the quay front (**43**), was a terrace wall dividing the waterfront area from the higher ground to the north. On that higher terrace, traces of the east edge of a new north-south road were recorded on the Fish Street Hill site, running parallel to a masonry-founded building of unusual plan. It was 14.6m (48ft) wide and at least 15m (49ft) long, north–south. The west wall, facing the street, may have supported columns or arches which led into a 1m (3ft) wide portico. Beyond that were at least six rooms, surfaced with brickearth. This building was built at the same time as the infilled quay to the south, since very similar groups of pottery were recovered from their respective construction levels. It is seen as part of a unified plan which saw a quay and transit sheds set up next to the new bridge: it may well have housed offices connected with the port and could therefore be interpreted as the Roman equivalent of the Custom House, in the heart of the commercial quarter. Opposite it, on the western side of the main road, further evidence for waterfront warehousing was recorded on the Miles Lane excavation as well as at Regis House, where imported samian ware pottery was being stored in a building which burnt down in the early second century. A similar dump of burnt, broken but unused samian ware was recovered from a building near Bucklersbury, in the Walbrook valley, in 1987.

Examination of finds from the town clearly

43 *A Roman harbour: timber-faced quay, drain and warehouse from the Pudding Lane site. The 10 x 100mm scale rests against the north wall of the warehouse; the 5 x 100mm scale is on the quay surface* (Museum of London).

show that a range of imports such as wine, dates, glass and marble from many parts of the empire found their way to London in this period, and passed through the network of trans-shipment centres that linked the provinces. Study of the storage jars from first- and second-century layers on the Pudding Lane site throws light on the port's traffic at this time. Some 80% of the vessels came from Spain and Southern France, with 52% being used to carry olive oil, 10% fish sauce, 10% wine, 6% the grape syrup known as defrutum, and 3% olives. The majority of the remainder had carried wine from other Mediterranean countries.

There was further extension of the waterfront in the mid-second century: that to the east of the

a)

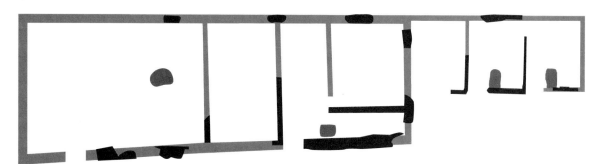

Building K

b)

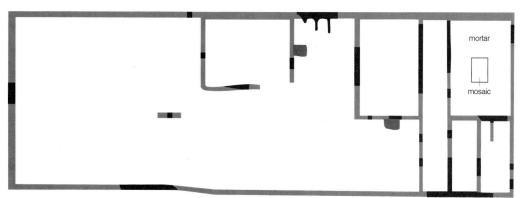

mortar

mosaic

Building F

c)

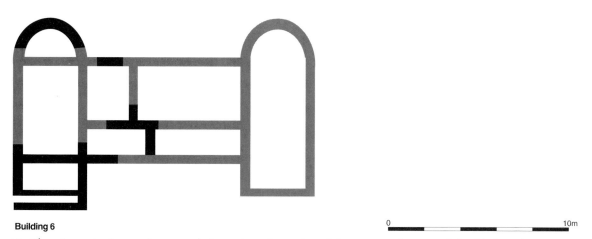

Building 6

0   10m

44 *Town houses in the second century: a) lower class: shop and workshop on street frontage to left, with domestic quarters to rear (Newgate Street site, Building K); b) middle class: well-appointed apartment block (Watling Court site, Building F); c) masonry-built bath-house, perhaps part of a small inn (Pudding Lane, Building 6)* (Chrissie Milne).

67

45 *The 2 x 100mm scale rests inside the plastered walls of a substantial residential building excavated in the snowy winter of 1978–9 at Watling Court* (Museum of London).

bridge incorporated post and plank revetments in modest extensions of less than 10m (33ft) southwards: these have been traced as far east as the site of the medieval Custom House. Immediately west of the bridge, the picture is different, for at Swan Lane a more robust quay was constructed with horizontally-laid timber baulks. The different treatment afforded sections of the contemporary waterfront shows that it may well have been divided into zones reflecting different activities or ownership.

New buildings

The remarkable mood of frenetic optimism which seems so characteristic of the AD 90s and 100s is detectable not just in the public building programme but in many of the individual town properties. Whereas only one of the two plots was developed in AD 90 on the Newgate Street site, by AD 100 buildings occupied both plots; at Watling Court the under-utilised area sees intensive development for the first time, as well-appointed residential buildings appear there (**44, 45**). At least one of the structures had a second storey, and evidence of early mosaic floor decoration was recorded. A notable find from the southernmost property was a military diploma issued in *c.* AD 100, presumably to an auxiliary veteran who had retired to live in Londinium. At Well Court just to the east, an insubstantial building was replaced by a more robust development of the street frontage, while new residential properties of some standing were built on the opposite side of the road, but set back from it. Many of these new buildings were of high quality: by the early second century, a timber-framed building at 33 Gutter Lane had a

46 *Private apartments. The 2 x 100mm scale rests on a tessellated pavement, cut by later pits, from a building recorded on the Whittington Avenue site in 1989* (Museum of London).

fine polychrome mosaic pavement set in an apsidal room, for example.

In the eastern half of the city, the pattern was the same: a timber building was replaced by a more substantial structure with courtyard at 88 Fenchurch Street, while to the east of the basilica the newly-widened road was lined with masonry-founded buildings with tessellated floors and painted wall plaster (**46**). The aisled hall excavated at 5 Fenchurch Street was also re-modelled in the early second century: one of the new rooms had an *opus signinum* (or *op. sig.–* a reddish concrete made from crushed tiles) floor and decorated walls, the design of which included a robed female figure (**colour plate 8**). There is also evidence of a taverna or shop on

the site, since a room contained five broken amphoras, storage jars which once contained wine from France, Italy, Greece and Rhodes, as well as fish sauce from Spain.

Contemporary developments on the south bank mirror those on the City shore, suggesting that Roman Southwark should not be seen as a subsidiary service settlement in this period, but as an integral part of Londinium. The waterfront was extended between AD 80 and 120, for example. Other early second-century redevelop-ments saw an industrial quarter laid out over the western part of the Courage Brewery site, complete with evidence of metal-working and a remarkably well-preserved timber structure, while to the east a new road was lined with residential buildings. On the Winchester Palace site, a large apsidal-ended masonry building of late first-century date is thought to be part of a public works programme. This was replaced in the early second century by a much larger complex extending over an area of at least 30m (98ft) east-west, incorporating two 10m (33ft) wide wings which led to another range directly overlooking the Thames. This well-appointed building seems to be associated with the provincial administration, since a third-century inscription records the presence of a military detachment here (see **78**).

A town transformed

The period AD 90–120 represents a time of spectacular growth for the Roman town: it had been replanned for the third time in half a century, but this time on a scale which quite over-shadowed the previous efforts. The town was now unequivocally a capital city, the largest in the land. It was fully furnished with public facilities, well-appointed private buildings (**47**) and was expanding in all directions. The governor and his administration were based here, and they saw the town rebuilt in keeping with its new role. The scale of investment is impressive: here was a clear vote of confidence in the future of Londinium. Alas, that confidence was to be short-lived.

47 *Preparing to lift the mosaic pavement from the Milk Street excavations* (Museum of London).

7

From Londinium to Augusta

A changing population

The population of Roman London did not grow gradually year after year, but suffered a series of sudden advances and major reverses. Over the last two decades, archaeological research has been directed at establishing the pattern and dating of this population change: for example, it is now suggested that the area of settlement within Londinium contracted in the late Roman period, and that the town was more densely populated in the early second century than it would be for another 1000 years. The evidence also suggested that the late Roman town contained a few masonry buildings of high quality set within a garden landscape with little evidence of the concentration of brickearth and timber structures which characterised the early town. The next problem to address was clearly one of explanation: what went wrong, or, to be less judgemental, why did these profound changes occur?

The broad answer must obviously lie, not within Londinium, but in a study of the province as a whole. There were profound changes taking place in the society and the economy: the apparent failure of towns like Londinium to maintain their momentum is but a reflection of that situation, rather than a cause of it. Nevertheless, since an understanding of the symptoms is the first step in a correct diagnosis of a disease, we should be absolutely clear about the archaeological evidence for when and how the population shrank. A full sequence of layers representing the complete span of Roman activity is not always recovered on excavations in London, since basements and other features have all too frequently cut away the later material. However, on sites where the latest Roman occupation layers have survived, be they second, third or fourth century, they are usually sealed beneath dark grey silts (**48**). These were noted by Professor Grimes in his post-war City excavations, by the DUA

48 *The Roman levels on this site in Newgate Street (now the headquarters of British Telecom) were sealed beneath a horizon of dark grey silts* (Museum of London).

during their campaign (**colour plate 12**), and by Harvey Sheldon's team working in Southwark. The resolution of the problem of late Roman London therefore devolved upon that horizon, and much research was devoted to understanding its formation and the interface between it and the underlying layers: this has been summarised in a recent paper by Brian Yule published in *Antiquity* in 1990.

Perhaps the principal problem which has dogged the understanding of the process is not the silts themselves but the use of the definite article to describe them: occupation levels were considered to be sealed by 'the' dark earth, which suggests that the same cause or a single event was responsible. The silts should not be seen as a Pompeii-like cloud of ash or lava which destroyed the city, rather each deposit should be considered separately on its own merits. Substantial horizons of grey silts have been recorded within Roman occupation sequences as well as above them: the date and manner of their formation on separate sites may well be different. This has been demonstrated by the work of soil scientists who have applied soil micromorphological techniques to the problem. This has shown that a dark grey silt could be produced by horticulture on some sites, the reworking of abandoned remains of brickearth and timber buildings on others, and the dumping of midden material elsewhere. Some deposits may even represent a combination of such factors. Each deposit therefore needs to be sampled and analysed independently to determine what it contains and how it formed.

That said, such dark earth deposits, however they were formed initially, do have a common property in that a soil once formed will serve as host to fauna such as worms. These creatures will then rework any malleable layers beneath the grey silts, converting them in turn into similar-coloured deposits. In other words, masonry walls and mosaic floors will survive beneath a grey silt horizon, whereas an abandoned mudbrick building and its earthen floors will not. Thus it is no surprise that the latest

Roman buildings which have been excavated in London were all substantial masonry structures: the phases of slighter structures which may have overlain them or existed alongside them simply cannot be expected to survive in a coherent form unless protected from the worm. This has already been shown on several sites where pits have clearly been cut from an unidentifiable surface within an otherwise homogeneous horizon of dark earth, as at the Newgate Street site, or at Foster Lane, where isolated patches of floor surfaces have only survived beneath grey silts where they have slumped into underlying pits, beyond the reach of the industrious worms. On such sites there is therefore a crucial distinction to be drawn between the date of:

a) the occupation sequence represented by the horizontally-bedded material, and

b) that represented by the pits, ditches, pottery and other artefacts recovered from the grey silts.

The latter may well be later than the former, but is no less important just because it is unaccompanied by building plans.

Having shown that the brickearth-based buildings of late Roman London would not have survived worm and root action, it therefore follows that calculations of the density of population in that town would be incorrect if they relied solely on the distribution of masonry structures. A count of surviving buildings on its own cannot therefore be used as a reliable guide to the density or duration of occupation in the town.

For resolution of this problem, attention turned to the pits, wells, bones and artefacts recovered from the late Roman levels. An initial study by Peter Marsden and Barbara West has produced useful results, but clearly more detailed work is urgently required to refine the conclusions, supported by a more precise dating framework. These caveats aside, they have compared early, middle and late Roman groups of material from a variety of sites in an attempt to suggest *relative* levels of population density in those three admittedly over-broad periods. For example, of the 114,000 spot-dates from over 300 DUA sites, 78% were dated to AD 50–150; only 7% were AD 150–270, with 15% AD 270–400. Of the 1.1 tonnes of animal bone examined from 26 City sites, 65% were from early Roman deposits, 7% from AD 150–270, while 28% were late Roman. Similar proportions were obtained for the distribution of wells from London and Southwark, with well over 60% cut in the first century of occupation.

Even allowing for the obvious bias towards the early material which such a general survey must have (first-century levels are far more likely to survive and be excavated than fourth-century ones), a consistent pattern seems to have emerged: the population of London was substantially reduced after AD 150, perhaps by as much as two thirds, but it may even have increased after the 270s. However, an argument against the broad thrust of this thesis is that it may reflect, not so much a change in the town's population as in its method of refuse disposal. Once convenient quarries and the Walbrook valley had been infilled with first- and second-century material, perhaps later Roman refuse was carted outside the walls and spread over more distant sites which have yet to be excavated, for example. Whatever the merits of this line of enquiry, it is clear that, although worms destroyed some of the buildings of late Roman London, they did not destroy the less digestible evidence of its population: the resolution of the problem concerning the town's fate may therefore lie in a detailed study of the contemporary artefacts (**colour plate 10**), stratified or not.

The late second- to third-century city

The town founded with such optimism in *c*. AD 90 did not maintain the momentum for rapid growth beyond the middle of the second century, if the studies discussed above are to be believed. Various explanations for this apparent decline have been proposed. For example, there is clear evidence for a damaging fire which swept through much of the western half of the town during the reign of the Emperor Hadrian, in the

120s. One tangible consequence of such disasters was the gradual adoption of more fire-proof masonry buildings throughout the city, for Londinium was beset by several fires during its life, some localised, others more widespread. While these may have been accidental, there is always the possibility that some may reflect political turmoil. Whatever the cause, the larger fires may have affected the settlement's ability to perform its role. Economic instabilities or the outbreak of the plague which ravaged much of Europe between AD 165–90 are other reasons cited in the continuing discussion of the apparent decline in the fortunes of late Roman London. However, it is possible that a more fundamental and long-term process of change was occurring, no doubt exacerbated by such superficially-damaging events.

The published evidence for occupation west of the Walbrook valley suggests that there were fewer buildings in that area beyond the late second century. Surveys of the material from the

49 *This late Roman mosaic pavement was discovered in 1934 during the extensive excavations on the site of the Bank of England. It was subsequently conserved and lifted and is now on display in the Bank's own museum (see fig. 80; no. 26) (Museum of London).*

73

more intensively settled eastern half of the town suggest the contraction came somewhat later there. Many of the industrial buildings in the Walbrook valley may have been demolished by the end of the third century: for example, the glass-working workshops recorded at 55 Moorgate had been abandoned by that date, sealed beneath thick demolition dumps. However some buildings such as those excavated at 4 Copthall Avenue, may have survived into the fourth century. Even public buildings were not exempt from this apparent spiral, since the prestigious Huggin Hill bath-house was systematically dismantled in the mid-second century, for example. However, its site was subsequently occupied by brickearth and timber buildings, an intriguing reversal of the standard development on most London sites. These structures, a relatively rare occurrence (or survival) for this period, were associated with some industrial activity and were

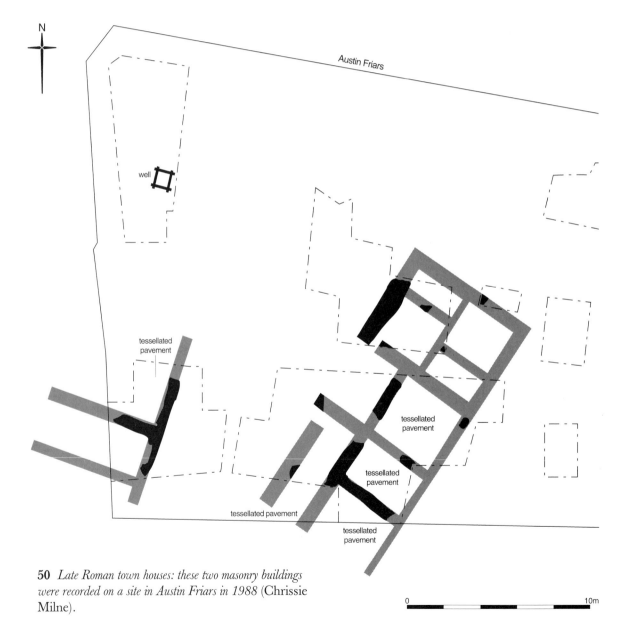

50 *Late Roman town houses: these two masonry buildings were recorded on a site in Austin Friars in 1988* (Chrissie Milne).

in use until the end of the third century.

This picture of apparent contraction and abandonment is but half of the story, for there is equally unequivocal evidence that a wealthy population, however small, was still in residence and that, by AD 200 at least, the town once more had the resources to mount public building programmes as required. A number of urban 'villas' of some pretension are already known from nineteenth- and early twentieth-century work in the City (**49**), such as that from which the Bucklersbury mosaic pavement was derived. More recent work since 1988 has added to that list. During the late second and third centuries, timber buildings were replaced by masonry on several sites, including 33 Gutter Lane, the apsidal-ended building on 4 Billiter Street, 80 Leadenhall Street and at 22 Austin Friars (**50**). On that site two new buildings were recorded: the eastern one had at least eight rooms, tessellated floors and painted plaster walls, with a courtyard to the west. Beyond that was another building, also with a tessellated floor and with a piped water supply. This period also saw such buildings erected on fresh sites: at Lothbury for example, part of a large urban 'villa' was erected just after AD 200. It had interconnecting rooms and a corridor ranged around a central courtyard. One room had an H-shaped hypocaust, painted wall plaster and a tessellated floor. This building continued in use with modifications well into the late Roman period. At the northern end of the City, a sequence of masonry buildings aligned on Bishopsgate was examined at 34 Great St Helens in 1992, an excavation interrupted by the first IRA bomb in the area. In the south-west, they have been recorded at 32, 40 and 61 Queen Street (**51**); on the latter site was a unique third-century arcaded building set just behind the contemporary waterfront.

Moving outside the town wall, a hurried excavation in 1988 near the Old Bailey recovered the plan of an octagonal building erected at the end of the second century overlooking the River Fleet: this has been interpreted as a Romano-Celtic temple, set between the two main

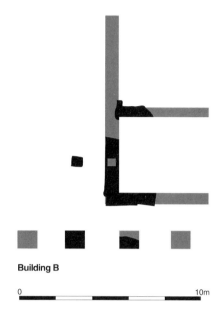

Building B

0   10m

51 *Part of an impressive arcaded building which overlooked the third-century waterfront. From the Queen Street site excavated in 1985–6* (Chrissie Milne).

roads heading westwards from the City. Of these roads, that leading from Ludgate was upgraded and now ran over the Fleet on a new bridge with masonry foundations. Another temple, the Mithraeum in the Walbrook valley, was erected in the 240s, by which time it seems that much of the south-west quarter of the town had already been adorned with spectacular buildings: the excavations at Baynard's Castle in 1975-6 uncovered the dismantled remains of a monumental arch, a screen of gods and an altar from a temple which had itself been restored at least once before being demolished for use in the riverside defensive wall. The published reconstructions show that early third-century London had been blessed by a spectacular range of buildings of real quality (**52**): remarkably, many of these would be demolished by the 270s.

Excavations to the east at St Peters Hill produced more monumental architecture, in the form of a prestigious complex that was begun in style and abandonded in haste (**colour plate 11**). It may have been up to 150m by 100m in size, and incorporated a structure built with blocks of

Lincolnshire limestone on a foundation some 3.5m (11½ft) wide, substantially wider than the landward city wall itself. Dendro-chronological samples from foundation piles which retained their sapwood and bark produced felling dates in the winter of AD 293 from those in the east, and the spring of 294 from those in the west (**53**). Thanks to the remarkable precision with which these piles have been dated, a rare conjunction of archaeology and history, it was possible to

suggest that the palatial building was raised on the orders of one Allectus. He was the governor of Britain from 293–6, having murdered the previous post-holder, and mounted an unsuccessful attempt to become Emperor. However, he was killed by a rival claimant in AD 296, and thus his monument was never completed. There is therefore evidence from the city of a series of impressive late third-century buildings, perhaps incorporating a palace, a mint and a treasury but built for a future which neither they nor their patron ever enjoyed.

This selective survey of the range of structures which were being built in third-century Londinium may thus be set beside the summary

52 *Embellishing the city. Reconstruction of a monumental arch, fragments of which (shown stippled) were found reused in the riverside wall near Blackfriars in 1976 (Sue Hurman, after S. Gibson).*

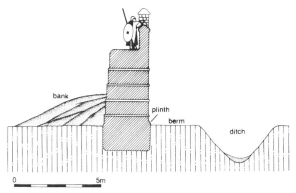

53 *Substantial masonry footings of an enigmatic structure on the St Peter's Hill site. The 10 x 100mm scale stands on the clay foundation level into which wooden piles were driven. Dendrochronological study of these piles dated the construction of the building to AD 293–4 (Museum of London).*

54 *Defending Londinium. A schematic cross-section through the early third-century city defences, showing the bank inside the defensive wall and the deep ditch outside it. The wall was constructed from ragstone rubble separated by four tiles courses, with a sandstone plinth at the base (Sue Hurman, after C. Maloney)*

of those which had been demolished previously: the picture which emerges is, yet again, one of profound change not just in quantity but in quality. However, before this century is passed over, there are two more major public work programmes which demand discussion and explanation: the wall and the waterfront.

Defending the city

One of the most costly works undertaken in Londinium was the construction of the 3km (2-mile) long landward wall between AD 190–220. The line and sheer bulk of this wall subsequently exercised a profound influence on the topographical development of the City, for it was 2.7m (9ft) thick at the base and would have stood over 6m (20ft) high (**54, 55**). Its structural details are now well known, but the reason for its construction is still the stuff of debate. It enclosed a far larger area than that intensively occupied at the time, as has been discussed above. Presumably its role was to provide protection, control or status for more than just the townspeople: its line was deliberately extended to take in the fort at Cripplegate, after which it

55 *Revealing the Roman city wall which survived behind plasterwork in the basement of a building demolished in Crosswall in 1980 (Museum of London).*

turned west then south to make use of the high ground overlooking the Fleet valley. Surprisingly for such a well-known monument, its precise alignment beyond Ludgate still remains uncertain, but it is thought to run south to the Thames.

The waterfront does not seem to have been enclosed by this wall, which seems strange for a defensive circuit. However, a new waterfront terrace was being constructed at precisely this period in the western half of the town, where felling dates of AD 196-7 have been obtained from timbers used in the quay excavated on the Vintry sites. This might imply that the defensive work was never finished through lack of resources or impetus. Alternatively it could be argued that the circuit was to be continued on the south bank around the Southwark settlement, an integral part of Londinium. However, no trace of such a masonry defence has been recovered from south of the river.

The historians' discussion as to the responsibility for the construction of the landward wall is still at present unresolved. If it was begun on the orders of the governor and usurper Clodius Albinus, then work must have started between AD 193-7. If it were the new emperor Septimius Severus, then a date after his arrival in Britannia in AD 208 might be more appropriate. This dispute will run until it is resolved by dendrochronology or a well-placed coin.

There have been many records made of the wall over the last century, and redevelopments continued to expose or damage it or its associated ditch in the 1970s and '80s. Nevertheless, substantial fragments of this monument survive to this day (see Chapter 12). A 12m (39ft) length was recorded standing to a height of 3m (10ft) above plinth level near Ludgate in 1982 which had been incorporated in the south wall of St Martin's church, and the extensive excavations at America Square revealed not only the wall, but also a metalled road which had been laid to facilitate its construction and which was sealed beneath the clay bank thrown up against its internal face. Even more recently, the Oxford

Archaeological Unit in 1993 examined a section of the Roman wall within the precinct of the Tower of London. It was integrated in the construction of the inner curtain wall and the Bowyer Tower, where it had been observed in 1911.

Apart from the two gates giving access to the Cripplegate fort, there were ultimately five main gates, at Aldgate, Bishopsgate, Aldersgate, Newgate and Ludgate. The foundations of the latter two were both glimpsed during recent watching briefs in 1985 and 1982 respectively. There may have been postern gates at intervals between the main exits: for example, a postern aligned on a known Roman road inside the walled area near Moorgate would have allowed access to the cemetery there.

For most of its length the wall was built on land beyond the occupied area, although occasional structures which antedate the wall have been recorded, such as the timber buildings on the Blomfield House site excavated in 1988. On the same site in the area of the 5m (16ft) wide ditch, a group of 500 coin moulds were found, thought to represent the activities of a late third-century forger. Interestingly, it was a hoard of similar 'irregular' coins of early third-century date found discarded in a tower on the wall near the Old Bailey which still constitute part of the prime dating evidence for the wall's construction. A convincing explanation of why coin 'forgers' were attracted to the town wall is needed. Perhaps the issue of such unofficial coinage was tolerated during periods in which regular money was in short supply.

Waterfront development

One of the prime reasons for siting Londinium on the Thames in the mid-first century was to take advantage of the tidal river, since it seemed to be founded at the contem-porary tidal head of the river. Vessels coming upstream could ride up on an incoming tide and then, having discharged their imported cargoes and loaded up with British produce, they could sail downstream on the next ebb tide. If the tidal head were to move away from London, then it would make more sense to move the port with it. It could be argued that this is precisely what happened in the late Roman period.

The study of river level change in London through the examination of Thames-side structures and related deposits is an important area of waterfront research, illuminating the history of the port as well as contributing to the wider studies of sea level change. The International Geological Correlation Programme's work on such changes in the United Kingdom has amassed much material concerning the last 10,000 years but, somewhat surprisingly, hasless data for the most recent 3000 years. Clearly the London evidence can make a major contribution to this particular discussion. As is now well known, south-east England has been gradually sinking since the retreat of the glaciers after the last ice age, some 10,000 years ago: quite independently of that, sea level has been rising. While the broad trend for both events is clear, there have been pronounced reversals in the sequence at times. One such reverse seems to have occurred in the Roman period, as research in the Thames estuary had already suggested, but the precise timing and long-term effects of that regression needed clarification. Close study of the waterfront has helped to illuminate this problem.

The development of the late Roman waterfront was one of the first tasks undertaken by the Guildhall Museum and then the DUA in the early 1970s, with the work at Custom House and Billingsgate. Nearly 20 years later, work in the other end of town was revealing further well-preserved sections of the last Roman quay at the extreme western end of the waterfront (**56**). As a consequence, our knowledge of the late second- to third-century phase is much fuller than that for the mid-second. Some areas were refaced with post and plank revetments as at the Swan Lane site in the late second century, others with the more substantial quays comprising horizontally-laid oak baulks. The openwork structure on the Old Custom House site falls into the latter

category, as do the late second- to early third-century infilled quays recorded near Billingsgate in the east and as far west as the Vintry. Again, as discussed in Chapter 6, it would seem as if these differences were reflecting differences of ownership or activity on the waterfront itself, although the scale of some of the extensions seems to carry the hallmark of public rather than private enterprise. The date at which the quays finally fell out of use is debatable, but seems to be in the late third century rather than the fourth. There were certainly no large waterfront projects constructed in the last century or so of Roman occupation after the 270s, a marked contrast to the frenetic activity of the previous two centuries.

A recent study of each phase of waterfront construction in London from AD 70 to AD 250 has shown that both the base and the top (in as much as it can be inferred) of each successive quay was laid at a lower level than its predecessor. This singular fact seems to support the assertion that the level of the Thames was actually dropping relative to the land during the Roman period: the figure may be as much as 1.5m (5ft) between the end of the first and the middle of the third century. This information can be compared with the level of occupation surfaces behind the first-century quay which could be at $c.$ +2m ($6\frac{1}{2}$ft) OD while the base of the late third-century riverside defensive wall seen to the east of Billingsgate Market was at +0.4m (1ft 4in) OD, a level considered to be well above the level of the Thames in AD 270. A similar drop of some 1.5m (5ft) is indicated.

If we are to accept these figures, then we must conclude that by that date, the river level had fallen too low to enjoy the effects of the tide: once the high water level fell to between –0.5m ($1\frac{1}{2}$ft) OD and –1m (3ft) OD, then the Thames would no longer be tidal in Roman London, since this was the level of the freshwater river on the (former) ebb tide. This level may have been reached by the late third century, at which time we can assume that the tidal head must have moved downstream. This alarming, almost

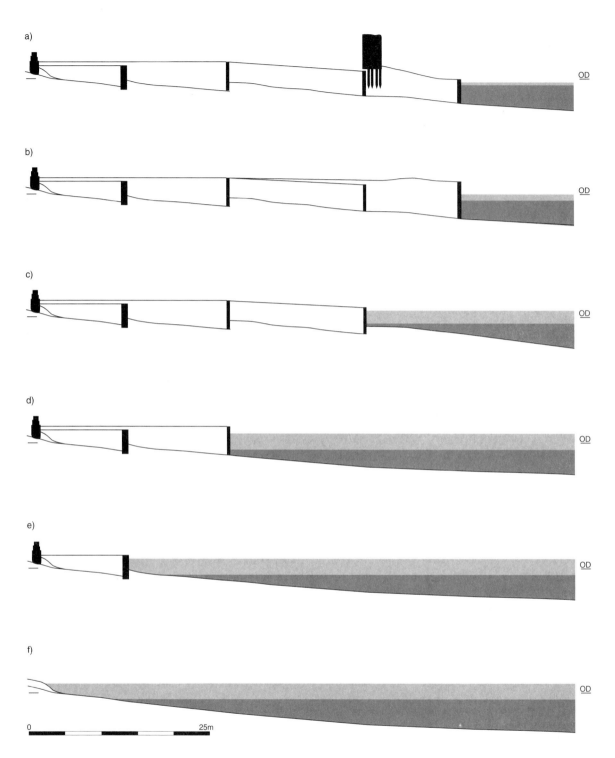

56 *Diagram showing Roman waterfront development from the first century (f), to the mid-third (b); after which the riverside wall was built (a). The dark tone marks the depth of water at low tide, the lighter tone the increased depth at high tide. Note how the tidal range (lighter tone) decreases over time* (Chrissie Milne).

visible rate of change in the river level during this period must, if true, have been a source of considerable confusion to the Romans. They were already working with an alien tidal regime (the tidal range in the Mediterranean basin is negligible) and now had to cope with falling river levels. The third-century engineers must have wondered why London was built where it was, once it no longer enjoyed the advantages of a tide-head town.

The suggestion of a falling river level provides a useful context in which to view the programme of waterfront extension in Roman London which began energetically in *c.* AD 70 and continued for almost two centuries. There is now therefore considerable evidence not just for one phase of extension, but for as many as seven stages in the development of the waterfront on some sites in the central zone near the bridge. That an area of up to 50m was reclaimed at the expense of the river requires explanation. Among the main reasons cited for such activity are: a) to win land; b) to provide a deep water berth; and c) to provide protection from flooding. Given the relatively undeveloped state of the nation in the first century, it seems at first glance that the winning of new land by such expensive means was not a cost-effective exercise. However, it should be pointed out that the hillside sloping down to the Thames was too steep to be readily habitable: the slope itself was subjected to major terracing programmes before it was fully developed, and much of the first-century quay could be seen as no more than an extension of that need.

As for the need to provide a deep water berth, it is suggested that, for that part of the waterfront where shipping needed to tie up, this was a major issue, and is reflected now in the changing level at which the bases of successive quays were built. There is clear evidence from the Old Custom House and Billingsgate sites that the third-century quays were deliberately laid out on the edge of the deep water channel itself, the presence of which was marked by a pronounced drop in the level of the foreshore at that point. Having advanced the waterfront as far south as

was possible, there was no more to be done with the quays if the river level continued to fall, although jetties could be built out and lighters could be used to service vessels moored in midstream. Nevertheless, it seems significant that maintenance of the quays stops at precisely the time they were rendered redundant by the falling river level and, in particular, the movement of the tidal head away from the city (**57**).

The port facility, the local trans-shipment centre, must have been moved elsewhere at this juncture. It is perhaps significant that a new settlement founded at Old Ford in Bow in the 270s flourished until the end of the Roman period. It lies at the junction of the main London–Colchester road and on the navigable River Lea, ultimately an outlet for material sent by barge from Verulamium. There may have been several such settlements on the junction of road and river crossings which benefited from the collapse of the port of London. As for the main entry ports in this period, these are likely to have been the coastal harbours which were being re-fortified, such as Dover, Richborough and Reculver. It is worth noting that the Dover fortification (and, therefore, presumably the harbour works which it protected) was moved from its first-century vantage point in the third century, suggesting that here too the effects of sea-level change were considerable.

Late third- to late fourth-century London

The great basilica suffered from an almost continuous programme of repair and modification throughout the second and third centuries: the last reconstruction followed a damaging third-century fire which caused the roof to collapse. Although the building was then reoccupied for a while, its days were numbered. The evidence from the recent excavation programme was unequivocal on this point: the building was not left as a derelict ruin, nor was its demolition piecemeal: it was systematic and total, the entire superstructure razed to the level of the contemporary ground surface, and the vast majority of the associated rubble carted away. The date for

57 *The remains of the early third-century quay, looking south towards the river. The Roman harbourworks were not maintained after the third century, but were allowed to fall into disrepair, as this example from the Thames Exchange site shows. Only the lower tiers of the front wall (beyond the 5 x 100mm scale) and one of the supporting braces have survived. The large circular pile once supported the multistorey carpark which occupied this site until 1988* (Museum of London).

its demise is within a decade or so of AD 300.

Already by that time, the buildings which had once lined the streets to north and east of the basilica had been demolished: as for the streets themselves, they had not been resurfaced since the mid to late third century, were covered in silt and increasingly cut by ruts and pot holes (**58**, **59**). Although the roads were still being used,

they were no longer being maintained, as once they had been with such vigorous regularity. A similar picture was seen on the roads in the west of the town: at Milk Street, the road, much deteriorated, was still in use until the late fourth century, although the roadside ditches had silted up a century before. At King Street, dark grey silts sealed both the latest road surface as well as a third-century building, although a fourth-century structure was found overlying the silts. The octagonal temple to the west of the city near the Old Bailey was replaced after AD 270 by a substantial masonry building with a hypocaust: this may represent another mansio, or inn for travellers, set as it was just outside the town wall. This building was in turn demolished sometime after AD 340.

58 *Public services were well maintained in early Roman London. Compare this well-prepared, early second-century street surface at Leadenhall Court with fig.* **59** *(10 x 100mm scale)* (Museum of London).

59 *This rutted late Roman road had not been resurfaced since* c. AD 275 *(10 x 100mm scale)* (Museum of London).

60 *Recording the eroded foundations of the late Roman riverside wall on the Baynard's Castle site in 1976. The south face of the wall to the right of the 10 x 100mm scale has been undermined by the Thames.* (Museum of London).

The settlement on the south bank at Southwark also saw major changes. By the late third century, the industrial zone on the Courage Brewery site had been abandoned, replaced by larger more substantial buildings. By the mid fourth, much of this residential area had been given over to a cemetery site, showing that much of Roman Southwark was now seen as an extramural area, and no longer an integral part of Londinium. However, the full extent of late Roman occupation has still to be determined. On the Winchester Palace site, a major building had been erected in the second century, perhaps as a residence for the governor or some of his staff. This suffered partial demolition in or by the early fourth century, although coin evidence suggests that some of the remaining rooms continued to be occupied into the second half of that century.

There is no direct archaeological evidence to mark the demolition of the bridge over the Thames. However, it has been shown that the dates of the votive coins recovered from the river after nineteenth-century dredging reach a final peak by the 320s, which could suggest that the bridge had been removed by AD 330, and replaced by a ferry. Although it could be argued that the lower number of later coins might suggest changes in religious practice, reflecting the rise of Christianity for example, evidence from the shrine at Bath shows that votive offerings to water deities did not decline there until after 368.

The spectacular Baynard's Castle excavation in 1975–6 convincingly demonstrated that the London waterfront was finally enclosed behind a defensive wall (**60**), contrary to some previous thought. However, the dating of the wall was initially thought to be fourth-century, until dendrochronological research showed that the work was actually late third-century. A number of other examinations of its alignment, including one within the Tower of London, have confirmed that broad date, although it seems that the work was carried out in separate sections over an extended period. Recent work on sites on both banks of the Walbrook confluence have shown that the river channel was further constrained and canalised to allow the wall to pass over it.

In 1974, excavations at Shadwell, a mile to the east of the City, revealed a mid- to late-third-century ditched enclosure in which was found a square masonry foundation some 8m (26ft) across. This is thought to represent a watch-tower or signal station, perhaps one of a series erected to guard the Thames approach to Londinium.

In the mid fourth century, a further addition was made to the defences when D-shaped bastions were added to the external face of the wall: these are thought to represent artillery platforms. Before the DUA began their work there was evidence for eleven such bastions on the eastern side of the City, but by 1980 it was

clear that there could have been as many as twenty-two, set at intervals of some 50m Examples have recently been located at 31 Jewry Street, The Crescent, Crosswall (**61**), St Mary Axe House and as far north as Blomfield House. They are associated with the infilling of the earlier V-shaped ditch and the cutting of a new U-shaped ditch further out from the wall. The solid base of these bastions was infilled with rubble and some contained fragments of funerary monuments (see **79**). These were derived from neighbouring cemeteries, perhaps those older parts which were not well maintained and had become overgrown, as parts of present-day Highgate cemetery are prone to do. An addition to the late third-century riverside wall was recorded within the precinct of the Tower of London, where a clay bank and a wall associated with eleven coins including a Valentinian II issue AD 388–92) was discovered. Late Roman London was clearly seen as worth defending.

61 *The rubble base of a bastion (with 10 x 100mm scale) projecting over an infilled ditch to the east of the Roman town wall, encapsulated within a nineteenth-century building at Crosswall* (Museum of London).

Augusta

That the settlements on both banks of the river contracted substantially in the third and fourth centuries is clear. Nevertheless, talk of a collapse or of impoverishment seems unjustified, for although the late Roman town was certainly smaller, it contained well-appointed private buildings as study of the waterfront area has shown. The building with its own bath suite excavated by the Guildhall Museum near Billingsgate is one well-known example. More recently, work on some neighbouring properties near Pudding Lane showed that a set of late-first-century warehouses had been converted into private dwellings by the late fourth century and a small inn which had been rebuilt as a private dwelling was subsequently rebuilt with an additional

62 *Town houses in the fourth-century: masonry buildings from a) the Lime Street site; from Pudding Lane in (b) the mid fourth and (c) the late fourth century* (Chrissie Milne). *See also fig.* **63**.

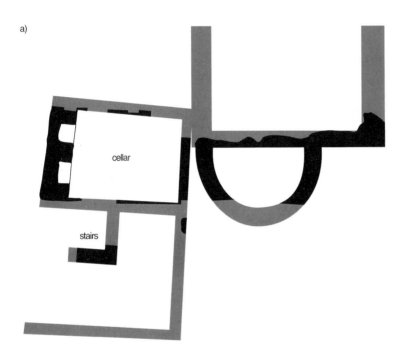

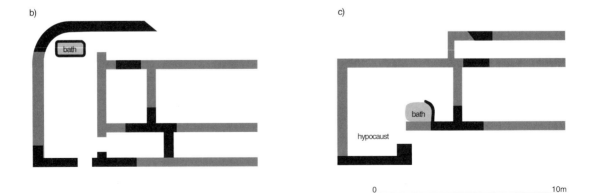

63 *Cleaning the hypocaust of a late Roman building at Pudding Lane* (Museum of London). *See also fig. 62c.*

hypocaust sometime after AD 350 (**62**, **63**). Further west at St Peter's Hill, part of the site of the possible palace of Allectus was occupied by domestic timber buildings from the mid to late fourth century. In the east, on a site in Pepys Street, part of a substantial aisled building was recorded which must be of at least late Roman date since it was built over deposits containing Portchester-D pottery. The density of the less robustly-constructed buildings which were also part of the contemporary town still needs to be fully assessed: the evidence lies in study of finds groups, pits and cemeteries rather than in the recovery of the foundations themselves, since these have survived but rarely. For example, the re-examination of pottery from the 1952 excavations at St Bride's church has just identified fifth-century material from a layer sealing a Roman

building, while on the opposite side of the City beyond Aldgate, recent excavations in the cemetery there discovered two fifth-century brooches accompanying a burial, while another grave had a chip-carved belt set and a gilt cross bow brooch of similar date.

Whatever the density or composition of residential buildings within the fouth-century town proves to be, it seems that Augusta (as Londinium was later known) lacked the wide range of public buildings that had graced the early Roman town. No public baths building has been found which could have served the third-century settlement and the harbour works were no longer maintained as a public facility beyond the 280s. Most of the roads suffered a similar fate, although a late-fourth-century coin was recovered from beneath the final surface of the Roman road beneath Cheapside. The amphitheatre continued to be used, however, but perhaps more as a market place than for official events, if the provisional studies are confirmed.

By the end of the fourth century, the south bank settlement had been abandoned and the shrunken north bank settlement was enclosed behind a robustly-constructed riverside wall, joined to the defensive landward circuit (**64**). It all seems a far cry from the optimism and expansion of the early second century. The role and status of Londinium had unquestionably changed again, quite as radically as it had in AD 70 or AD 90. Once more, the catalyst could be sought in external factors. In the first and second centuries the system of government developed by the Roman administration demanded that magistrates and members of the *ordo*, the local council, should live in their town: as a consequence, that settlement provided the trappings and facilities of civilised living which such a class required. By the fourth century, that level and style of local government had largely been replaced by a vast, centralised imperial system of direct administration. No longer legally obliged to live in towns, the local officials could concentrate on other matters, such as their country estates. For Londinium the result was dramatic: the trappings of obsolete local government such as the great basilica, were abandoned, while the maintenance of public facilities such as the city streets, all but ceased. Only work on the defences continued. Late-fourth-century London was a prosperous, self-sustaining nucleated settlement of no great size. It was concerned with administration and tax collection, and may have accommodated a periodic market. But it was neither a bustling port nor a centre of industry. The emperor Hadrian would not have recognised it as a town at all.

Continuity?

When the Department of Urban Archaeology was established in 1973, all the talk was of 'continuity': it was widely assumed that life continued in some form within the late Roman town of Londinium throughout the Dark Ages, and that 'the mart of many nations' described by the Venerable Bede in the 730s was the direct

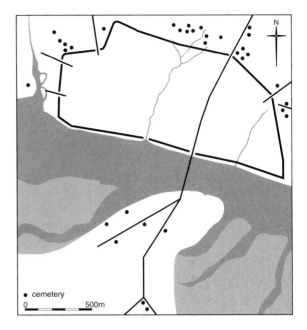

64 *Plan showing the line of a late Roman defensive wall on the north bank, with a scatter of cemetery sites outside it. It is not known precisely how much of the interior was occupied in the fourth century* (Chrissie Milne).

descendant of the settlement once destroyed by Boudica. Martin Biddle echoed Sir Mortimer Wheeler's words that there was 'a continuing if unexalted, civic consciousness in London throughout the fifth and sixth centuries ... it was either conquered by the English or (and this is perhaps more likely) passed peacefully under their control after a long period of cultural assimilation.' All the archaeologists had to do was find the evidence to prove it.

The DUA did their best. The open area excavations advocated as the best means of identifying late and sub-Roman deposits were universally adopted from the outset. The first problem encountered was that many of the Roman sequences excavated were truncated by modern basements, so that it was not possible to be sure how long occupation lasted on that particular site. Nevertheless by 1982 it had become clear that the latest Roman occupation horizons seemed to be late second century on many sites in the western part of the city, late third or early fourth on some sites around the forum area, and late fourth or early fifth on some parts of the waterfront terrace. Worse news was to come, for whenever untruncated late Roman occupation sequences were recorded, as on the Pudding Lane sites, they were found to be sealed by deposits of dark grey silt which were in turn cut by pits or sealed by building containing pottery, not of early or mid-Saxon date, but no earlier than the late ninth or tenth century.

On the waterfront itself, the stratigraphic sequence develops southwards rather than vertically, and thus if convincing evidence for continuity was to be recovered anywhere in London, then it would be found there. By the same token, if the waterfront provided unambiguous evidence for abandonment, which it did on the St Magnus House sites in 1974-5 for example, then that message had to be accepted. The Roman quays were not maintained or repaired in the fourth century: they were sealed beneath foreshore deposits over which waterfront embankments were raised, not in the fifth to ninth centuries, but in the period after AD 900. All the archaeological evidence therefore points to the Roman settlement contracting and finally failing in the fifth century, but reviving in the late Saxon period some 400 to 500 years later. The archaeological evidence seemed as damning as it was conclusive: London did not survive into the mid-Saxon period, and the bustling emporium described by Bede seemed alarmingly fictional. Still unable to believe the evidence of their own research, the DUA set up a major excavation on the Billingsgate Lorry Park site in 1982–3 specifically to find the elusive Dark Age harbour

once and for all. We were looking in the wrong place.

The following year saw perhaps the single most important discovery that has transformed our perception of the Roman town. This was the realisation that the mid-Saxon (seventh- to eighth-century) settlement of Lundenwic lay outside the old Roman walls, to the west of the city, in the Aldwych. Credit for this lies initially with Martin Biddle and Alan Vince and subsequently with the team from the Department of Greater London Archaeology, whose excavations in advance of redevelopments in the Covent Garden area produced the incontrovertible evidence for the lost chapter in London's history. The mid-Saxon settlement was a new foundation on a new site, a development independent of any direct classical antecedent. At a stroke, this discovery not only explained away the dearth of mid-Saxon material within the City, but also removed the rationale for the continuity argument once and for all. Certainly the city wall survived as a conspicuous landmark in the sixth century: within its confines, perhaps the earth-work of the amphitheatre would have been visible, as would the ruins of some of the later Roman masonry buildings: farms there may have been: town life there was not.

Once it became clear that the Roman settlement did not have to linger on for centuries to attract the attention of seventh-century Saxons, Londinium could die in peace in the fifth century, as the archaeological evidence had long attested. No British settlement can boast a continuous urban ancestry older than mid-Saxon: London is no exception.

8

Answers and questions

Previous chapters have outlined some of the results of the DUA's excavations: among the more spectacular discoveries were the riverside wall (1976), domestic buildings on the Newgate Street and Watling Court sites (1978–9), the bridge and harbour complex (1981), the Basilica (1986), the amphitheatre (1987) and the Huggin Hill bath-house (1989). However, there were many more discoveries than those which hit the headlines, for the real value of a site cannot be judged on the column inches it merits in the national press. Indeed, the major contribution which the DUA made to the archaeology of Roman London was not any one particular site but the sheer number of excavations which it recorded and the stratified groups it recovered. Many significant discoveries and insights into Londinium have yet to be made, for they still lie locked within the archive: indeed, the next generation of London archaeologists should not work on building sites, but on the vast database already collected, on the structural sequences, the finds groups, the seeds and the bones. It is a legacy that will be drawn on for a century or more, a legacy which London should treasure.

In this book, a personal assessment has been made of the DUA's contribution to the discovery of Londinium, while stressing that this contribution will increase as more raw data are researched and published. What can be said already is that the picture of the Roman town drawn from the evidence collected over the last 18 years has changed from that presented in the late 1960s.

Sometimes the recent work has revealed whole sections of Londinium which had been previously unknown: for example, the harbour area or the amphitheatre. In addition, there are also many changes in detail, as the sheer mass of recent excavations must dictate, but this wealth of data has substantially benefited our understanding of the origins, topography, extent, status, ethnic mix, development, fabric and chronology of the settlement. Once the form of the town is clearly understood, then its function and role can be interpreted more easily. We now have sufficient evidence collected to begin a reappraisal of the changing role of Londinium, measuring the weight of the archaeological sequence against the threadbare documentary record reviewed in Chapter 1.

Of paramount importance is that a detailed chronology for the development of the city is now being established: it may soon be possible to produce phase maps of Londinium's growth at 10- or 25-year intervals, a powerful tool with which to understand the dynamics of urban development. The origins, chequered develoment and final phases of the town would all benefit from such study. It would also be instructive to compare the phasing of activity on the north bank with developments in the contemporary settlement in Southwark, for example, leading to a reassessment of the relationship between both areas. Should the southern settlement be seen as an ancillary suburb, or does the discovery of high quality buildings there suggest it was an integral part of Londinium? Comparative studies with settlements in its hinterland and with other towns will also prove instructive.

A 'Governor's Palace' demolished

Sometimes buildings recorded before 1973 have been reinterpreted in the light of the DUA's efforts. Work on the basilica began in 1880, for example: over the next century there were seventeen investigations in the area. As a consequence, the current interpretation of its form and chronology is significantly different from that previously held (**65**). These new interpretations of what the building looked like change our view

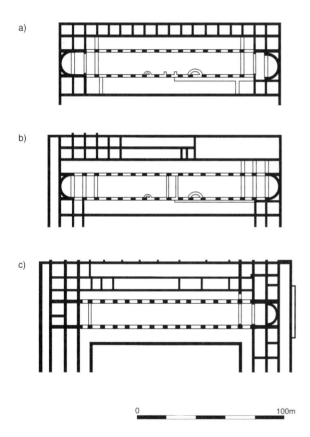

65 *As more information is collected, so our understanding of Londinium is extended. This example shows how our appreciation of the form of the second-century basilica has altered dramatically, changing our ideas of how the building was actually used: the basilica according to: a) G. Dunning in 1931; b) P. Marsden in 1987; c) T. Brigham in 1991* (Chrissie Milne).

of how it was intended to function, as well as how it was ultimately used.

There have also been occasions when previously-held interpretations have been completely overturned. An example is that of the so-called Governor's Palace, a complex of buildings investigated between 1961 and 1972 off Cannon Street. Substantial masonry walls, associated with painted wall plaster, fragments of mosaic pavements, *opus signinum* floors and hypocaust systems were recorded over a wide area. When this work was brought together for publication in 1975, the remains were interpreted as those of the palace of the provincial governor of Britannia. This identification was based on a number of criteria, of which the more important were that the extensive spread of walls represented contemporary developments and was an integral part of a single structure in which evidence of symmetry could be recognised. The size of this unified complex was extensive, some 130m north–south and 100m east–west and, according to the excavator, its plan was similar to that of buildings identified elsewhere as palaces, such as at Fishbourne in Sussex. It was then suggested that the most likely owner of such a large waterfront palace in London would be the provincial governor.

The so-called palace was thought to have comprised four ranges set around a courtyard: the east and west wings extended northwards towards the Roman road following the broad line of Cannon Street itself, while a separate but related courtyard complex lay immediately east of it. However, the published plans clearly show that the north and east wings are not structurally integrated: indeed, the walls are of glaringly differing thickness and alignments; the east wing does not line up happily with the apse to the north, but seems to be of a markedly different phase for example. The south and east wings are clearly not structurally integrated, but butt against each other as though they represent two discrete but neighbouring properties built at different dates. Given the wide divergences in levels on this hillside site, it is hard to see how mutual

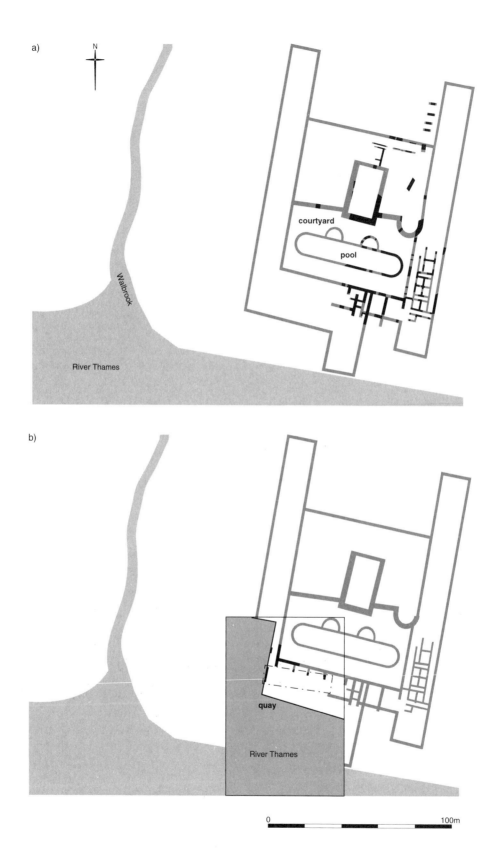

access between the wings would have been achieved: just taking the published evidence at face value, it would seem that a group of quite separate properties are represented.

The final proof that the palace was not all it once seemed came in 1988–9 when the DUA conducted extensive rescue excavations over the site of the projected south and west wings. On the western side of the site a large timber-built quay was recorded, which ran north–south along the edge of the River Walbrook whose bank lay much further east than had been anticipated: in fact there was no 'west wing' of the palace at all, since that area was occupied by the revetted mouth of the Walbrook (**66**). There was also a substantial retaining wall running across the site, dividing an area of higher ground to the north from the lower levels to the south. This area therefore proved to be an open terrace devoid of major buildings which, in the words of the excavators, did 'not accord with earlier interpretations of the area as having been occupied by the southern wing of a palace'. While it remains clear the spread of walls in the Cannon Street area do represent a major Roman redevelopment or redevelopments, it is decidedly not a palace on the lines suggested in 1975.

That London's archaeology is subject to radical revision should not be a matter of concern: it is not the worth of the original fieldwork which is being questioned, merely the interpretation of it. The residence in which the provincial governors lived when in Londinium has yet to be identified, and a number of contenders have already been proposed, ranging from Cripplegate fort itself to a well-appointed building excavated in Southwark on the Winchester Palace site. It has also been suggested that there was a late third-century palace built, or rather started, for Allectus in the St Peter's Hill area. We can now

turn our attention to discovering its late first- to second-century predecessor, if such there ever was.

With the hindrance of hindsight

Just how the story of Londinium has been interpreted also deserves some comment. An attempt has been made to determine, not just how large London became, but how successful the settlement actually was, the extent to which it met the expectations of the Imperial planners. What is clear is that the history of Roman London has many eventful chapters. Indeed, the changes are so marked that it is best to think of Londinium not as one town, a view subconsciously fostered by the bestselling Ordnance Survey Map of Roman London, but as a *series* of towns, each one overlying the other. Viewed from the well-ordered shelves of the Guildhall Library, a clear and seemingly inevitable pattern can be traced through this 400-year period: foundation, expansion, change, contraction, decline and ultimately, fall. Such developments could be described and discussed the more easily because we know what happened next, the hindrance of hindsight. This is a luxury which was not afforded the original citizens, and one which must be avoided if real insights into the development of that town are to be gained.

London, like Rome, was not built in a day. It was a town like many others, a speculative venture, founded as a symbol of confidence in the future: it might succeed, it might survive; it might succumb, but only the former proposition was in the minds of its founding fathers. Given that every phase in the town's development was planned with a particular view of the future in mind, then each phase can be said to encapsulate within its design a prospect of the future as it seemed to the contemporary inhabitants. Rather

---

66 *Changing interpretations of Roman London: a) suggested plan of 'Governor's Palace' in London in relation to the position of the mouth of the Walbrook, based on data available in the 1970s. Conjectured wall alignments are shown toned; b) schematic plan of London 'Palace' and Walbrook mouth (cf., fig. **66**a) shown in the light tone. The inset superimposed on the latter shows the position of the substantially wider Walbrook mouth, based on results from the excavations below Cannon Street Station in 1988–9* (Chrissie Milne).

than a logical and inevitable progression, the series of redevelopments which make up the story of Roman London can therefore be seen as a series of statements of intent. As such they provide yardsticks with which to measure the success of each phase of settlement, given that a successful episode in the history of the town would be the one which best meets the expectations of its founders or developers.

Consider these questions: why were there no defences around Londinium before the AD 60 uprising? Why bother to build such a large bath-house at Huggin Hill which was used for less than 30 years? Why did the City wall enclose such an extensive area in AD 200, so little of which was subsequently occupied? Why were the harbour works extended in AD 250, when they silted up almost immediately? An answer to all these could be the same: because the Romans did not know what happened next, and were actually planning for a different future, or, more correctly, a different series of futures, not all of which came to pass. The forum laid out in AD 75 presents a modest, unexceptional prospect for the second-century town, while the later much enlarged civic centre shows a more robust view of Londinium's role for the succeeding years. We now know that the path which London actually took differed quite markedly from that planned out for it on both those particular occasions. It performed better than expected in the first instance, and under-achieved in the second.

Londinium does not seem to have been in charge of its own destiny, but was a hostage to the fortunes of Rome. As such, its chequered development presents a mirror in which we can observe those changes in the Imperial policy for Britannia as a whole (**67**). The evidence laid out in the previous chapters clearly shows how the form and status of Londinium changed. The town did not grow coherently from a pre-determined focus but was in effect replanned on more than one occasion. The archaeologist can therefore show when and how London changed and can go on to suggest what *role* it may have performed in a particular century; it is up to

classical historians to deduce what precise legal *status* such a settlement might have enjoyed, be it *municipium*, *colonia* or whatever.

To sum up: the supply base of the 50s was principally a ribbon development: it developed along the road running from the west country to Camulodunum on the banks of the Thames above a ferry crossing giving access to the south coast ports. It is suggested that the potential of the site became clearer as the invasion and occupation of the province proceeded apace and, as a consequence, the nucleus was then deliberately replanned as a modest settlement with a rectangular grid of streets on Cornhill. It was this town, still in the process of being built which was sacked in AD 60. When rebuilding finally commenced, it was on the lines already drawn up, but greater resources were made available, for masonry public buildings are readily identifiable for the first time. The AD 70s were a period of military expansion: the frontier was being moved forward, its supply lines back in full use. However, no sooner was the first London forum completed than work on a much larger complex began around it by AD 90–100, showing that the town's function had changed yet again.

It seems clear that there was a major reorganisation of the province at the end of the first century, after the battle of *Mons Graupius* in AD 84 which saw the defeat of the British in the bellicose north. That was a time for taking stock, since it was only *after* this date that the true extent and potential of the hard-won province could be assessed accurately. A design for the administration of the enlarged province was then drawn up in which, it seems, the role of Londinium was destined to loom large. The town lay in the heart of the safe south, astride what became the main land route to the north: it was also within reach of the sea and Channel ports, the primary gateways for supplies and communications, and a convenient means of escape should the need arise again. The construction of the enlarged basilica in London together with the attendant urban expansion is therefore seen as a reflection of the increased importance of that

67 *London's changing administrative responsibilities: a) the first provincial capital was at Camulodunum (Colchester) but by AD 90 (b), London had taken over that role for a much-enlarged province. When the province was subdivided in AD 200 (c) and AD 300 (d) the extent of London's responsibilities shrank dramatically, only to expand again in the late fourth century (e)* (Chrissie Milne).

town in the late-first-century scheme for the development of Britannia. This saw the province administered not from Camulodunum, inconveniently situated to the east of the principal road routes of the recently enlarged province, but from Londinium, at the hub of that expanding communications network.

The establishment of Londinium as the most powerful town in the province can now be dated to AD 85–90, in the reign of the emperor Domitian (AD 81–96). This new city, rebuilt with all the confidence of a Canary Wharf, ultimately failed to maintain the expected momentum. Contraction and change followed: the late Roman town was stripped of its public buildings as the local administration was replaced by a more distant authority. Nevertheless, the newly-named Augusta should not be considered as an impoverished ghost town. Indeed, the actual extent of the late Roman town is still a matter of debate, since the cutting of deep cellars all too often removed evidence of fourth-century occu-pation, while on the few sites which were blessed with shallow basements,some of the very latest occupation levels seem to have been reworked and destroyed by worm and root action.

It is possible that one reason for the assumed contraction of Roman London might be sought in the events of the 280s and 290s, when Londinium and the governor led an unsuccessful rebellion against Rome. It is possible that the town, if strongly identified with the usurper Allectus, may have been punished: a consequence may have been the demolition of its great basilica, for example, or Cripplegate fort with its garrison. Once the lesson had been learned, the town may have found favour with the authorities once more, and been reinstated

with the title of Augusta in the late fourth century. Such a suggestion, it must be admitted, is but speculation. What seems more certain, however, is that London subsequently failed as a port, although the precise rate of river level change must be more clearly assessed, and the effect on the workings of the harbour more closely evaluated. It also saw its role as provincial capital eroded, as the provincial administration was subdivided in c. AD 200 and again in c. AD 300 – when the military capital was based at York (or Eburacum) – although it is argued that it retained a supervisory view over the other new sub-provinces of Britannia. There was also a more widespread decline in the provision of public facilities in the late Roman period as the magistrates and local council were no longer obliged to live in towns. When set against this litany of lost roles, the contraction and change undergone by late Roman London seems positively modest.

It is not therefore possible to plot a seamless development of this ancient town: what can be done is to identify the chronology of the principal phases in the city's development, and then to pause at each juncture and interpret that phase, considering the form and function of the settlement itself and its contemporary role in the province. The development of the provincial capital can thus be examined from the standpoint of the changing expectations of the Roman administration. The Romans could impose their will upon the present with the construction of roads, buildings and basilicas, but for all their military might and engineering expertise, they could not dictate the future. Since they were obliged to rebuild Londinium several times, we may conclude that for Roman London, things rarely went according to plan.

9
Rebuilding Londinium

Towards a three-dimensional townscape

London archaeologists have devoted much time to the recording of the plans, that is the outline, of Roman buildings, simply because the associated superstructure rarely survives. As a consequence our understanding of the town and its development tends towards a two-dimensional history. Such an approach, while understandable in the circumstances, fails to appreciate the reality of three-dimensional settlement, which provides a very different picture. Take, for example, the plan of St Paul's Cathedral: it clearly represents a large building, but the mere outline on its own cannot convey the height of the church, or the impression of space enclosed within the shell, or that it is crowned with a dome and the impact which that feature has on the skyline. To understand the Roman townscape the archaeologist must be prepared to think in three dimensions and to attempt as many reconstructions as the evidence will allow. In this chapter, four exercises in reconstruction are summarised. Two are on paper, one has materialised as a scale model in a museum, while the last one is full size and for real, the ultimate test. Such projects do more than make the past more understandable to an uncompre-hending public: their real virtue is that they teach the uncomprehending archaeologist pre-cisely what is possible and practical. Indeed, reconstruction is a tough and uncompromising teacher, but one from whom as much can be learned by the reconstructor as by the observer.

A timber-framed building

The most common structures in Londinium were not masonry buildings with mosaic floors, as was commonly thought, before detailed excavation showed otherwise. Buildings made with mudbricks or timber elements were the norm, especially in the first two centuries. However, although over 200 such vernacular houses have been recorded since 1973, the evidence is usually confined to the floors and foundations, and occasionally the stubs of the walls themselves. Nevertheless, recent work has shown that a particular class of building which incorporated squared timber base-plates was present in the town, represented on some sites by a beam slot or an impression of the decayed timber. The evidence gathered from desiccated sites therefore suggested that the Romans made use of a form of timber-framed building; a suggestion subsequently confirmed by the recording of sill-beams or base-plates which actually survived *in situ,* with square mortices cut in the upper face, on water-logged sites such as at Copthall Avenue, in the Walbrook valley. One of the vertical members, called studs, which would have been set into such base-plates, was recovered from reclamation deposits on the waterfront at Pudding Lane and showed that Roman timber-framing bore only a superficial resemblance to the construction techniques of the late-medieval period. Even more spectacular was the structure recorded in 1988 in Southwark on the Courage Brewery site, which had base-plates, joists, floor boards, and a base of collapsed wall-posts with plank cladding attached.

However, the reconstruction considered here is based on a study of twenty-two of the piles found beneath a late-second- or early-third-century stone wall on the excavations below Cannon Street station in 1989. Although the timbers had been cut up and their ends tapered, Damian Goodburn identified them as reused house timbers, and with his customary insight was able to piece together the building tradition they represented. Samples taken for dendro-chronological study showed that all these piles were from trees between 25 and 65 years old. Since at least eleven of the oaks had been felled at the same time, this suggests that the timbers were probably derived from the same framed building (**68**).

Among the structural elements represented were ten plates, six studs, one corner-post, three diagonal braces and a top-plate, from which Damian was able to reconstruct much of the carcass of the associated frame. First, the base-plates were laid and then the long thin tenons on

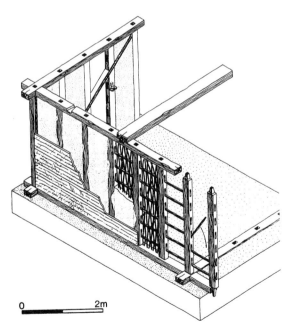

68 *Partial reconstruction of a Roman timber-framed building, based on evidence from reused timbers found on the Cannon Street site* (Damian Goodburn).

the feet of the studs and corner-posts were set into square mortices some 0.6m (2ft) apart which passed through the thickness of the plate. Lateral strength was provided by diagonal braces lapped over the studs, although this may have been confined to the corners. The height of the wall was calculated on the length of the studs, and would have been some 2.4m (8ft) tall. Sloping recesses in the edges of the studs would have allowed for the insertion of slighter horizontal members around which laths would have been woven to provide a panel which would have been covered in brickearth daub. However, the internal faces of the plates and vertical elements seem to have been left exposed. Horizontally-laid top-plates articulated with the heads of the vertical members, and one of these plates had the housing of a lap dovetail joint cut into it, showing that a tie-beam passed across the width of the building at top-plate level. The pattern of nails and nail-holes recorded on the outer face of the studs shows that the building was clad externally with planks up to 350mm (14in) wide and up to 30mm (2in) thick, laid edge to edge. This outer skin provided further protection both from the weather and from potential intruders as well as giving the frame additional stability. The opposite face of two of the studs were charred over a small area, the mark forming a candle flame silhouette from an oil lamp placed on a bracket which had burned close to the timber. One of the lamps had been set 1.26m (4ft) above the baseplate, and would therefore have provided general lighting for the room, but the other was set only 0.56m (2ft) above the contemporary floor, perhaps suggesting that the occupant needed light while working seated on the floor or a low stool.

Forum and basilica

The next project moves from vernacular single-storey structures to the largest building in Londinium, the great basilica and forum upon which construction began in *c*. AD 90. Work at the Leadenhall Court and Whittington Avenue sites has added considerably to the evidence for both the external and internal appearance of the basilica. Working from the revised ground plan, Trevor Brigham attempted a reconstruction of this remarkable building from floor to roof line, and his work is summarised here (**69**). First, the field records were analysed to determine the order of construction and to establish the complex sequence of development. Then an accurate, scaled ground-plan of the basilica was compiled, after which consideration turned to the superstructure. Although there are obvious problems in determining the number and height of storeys in any building when working only from a ground plan, study of it shows that multi-storey buildings were commonplace in Britain, the evidence coming in the form of features such as unusually broad foundations, additional buttresses and small rooms serving as stairwells. Following these criteria, it is clear that the dimensions of the basilica foundations and superstructure and the presence of buttresses were significant to the form of the building. Thus although a particular wall taken in isolation cannot be used to demonstrate a particular height of the associated superstructure, the existence of a range of widths implies that there was internal con-sistency to the design. Having established this, it is possible to suggest a corresponding range of wall heights. The presence of buttresses suggests the direction of thrust of various walls, and therefore the direction of the roof in that partic-ular area.

The east–west walls of the basilica were more substantially constructed nearer the nave, presumably in proportion to the increasing height of the building. The walls which crossed the 14m (46ft) width of the nave had to carry the additional burden of gables and the central roof ridge without the aid of buttresses, and it was here, consequently, that the thickest walls were constructed, with the most massive separating the apse from the main body of the building. The latter must have supported both the main basilica roof, that of the apse itself, and the end gable.

The approximate height of the basilica can be calculated working from a constant set of values.

A reconstructed cross-section through the basilica, with a roof-pitch of 1:2 (around 25 degrees), clerestories of a minimum 1.5m to 2.5m (5 to 8ft), and a minimum height for the northern street-frontage of 3.5m to 4m ($11\frac{1}{2}$ to 13ft), gives a height of 25m to 26m (82 to 85ft) for the apex of the nave roof. Significantly, the height of the nave would seem to have been one quarter of its length and twice its width.

Given the increasing widths of foundation and superstructure through the northern range, north aisle and nave, it seems that the roofs of these areas rose in a series of tiers, allowing each interior to be lit by clerestories. The extra width and buttressing of the northern external wall suggests that some of the load was also dispersed outwards through the series of cross-walls dividing the offices and possibly through vaulting in the street-front rooms. The apse almost certainly had its own half-domed or conical roof, and its presence was further stressed by the later addition of an eastern portico, projecting 3m (10ft) beyond the adjoining eastern range. The east wall of the portico probably carried a low colonnade to support the roof.

Most of the tile used in the basilica was supplied by tileries in Hertfordshire and North Kent. The roof was of plain red tile, although the nave and western antechamber were partly covered by white tile, slipped red in order to resemble standard *tegulae* (an expensive device which suggests that a repair was required). Examples of these tiles were recovered from collapsed sections of the roof. There is little evidence to suggest that the basilica was decorated externally. The grey of the ragstone would have contrasted with the regular red brick courses and roof. Lintels, and the dressing of windows, doorways and quoins were probably also executed in brick.

Initially, the public rooms were probably provided with raised timber floors but most of these were replaced by *opus signinum*. The rooms opening onto the streets had brickearth and mortar surfaces, while there was a herringbone-pattern (*opus spicatum*) tiled pavement in the eastern

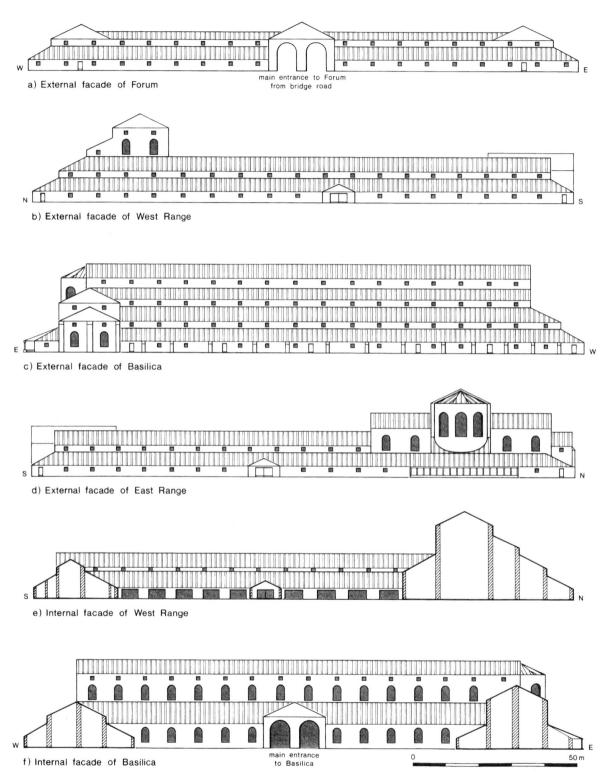

a) External facade of Forum

main entrance to Forum
from bridge road

b) External facade of West Range

c) External facade of Basilica

d) External facade of East Range

e) Internal facade of West Range

f) Internal facade of Basilica

main entrance
to Basilica

0   50 m

69*a-f Elevations of basilica* (Susan Banks).

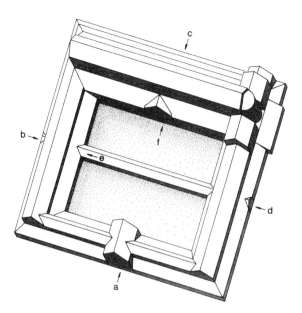

69g *Projection of basilica showing location of elevations a-f* (Susan Banks)

portico and a tessellated pavement in one of the offices. *In situ* evidence for interior decoration includes dark-blue painted plaster from the dado level in one room, mixed painted panels in another and a 50mm-thick plaster coat in the apse, perhaps for an inlay surface. Study of the wall plaster recovered from various destruction deposits showed that great efforts were made to lighten the public rooms, while the eastern ante-chamber was intended to be a contrasting and striking focal point, leading the eye towards the apse, which was painted with human figures at one stage. The offices were given different colour schemes while the street-front range was normally red and white.

As for the rest of the second-century forum complex, the south, east and west wings initially comprised three ranges set around a courtyard, with an extra inner range added subsequently. The three main ranges seem to have comprised two ranges of shops or offices with an outer portico, which suggests a high central range spanning the rooms, and a lower roof to the portico. This would have been mirrored by a lean-to roof on the extra inner porticos. The height of the porticos and the central range were

probably comparable with that of the street-front rooms and offices of the basilica's northern range. The position of the forum opposite the road to the bridge, and the known elements of the layout, combine to suggest that there was a central entrance in the south range. The side walls of the entrance were 20m (66ft) apart in all, although the opening itself was presumably narrower, perhaps an arch of a similar width to those spanning the basilica nave. The only other entrances may have been in the side walls, which would have been secured at night or during disturbances. These doors opened into the central east–west walkway which divided the courtyard, a colonnaded feature which would have provided covered access across the complex in all weathers. It represents one of several notable reinterpretations of the structural evidence by Trevor Brigham: the foundations had initially been seen as part of an ornamental pool in the centre of the courtyard.

London's bridge

The road from the forum led south to the head of the bridge over the Thames, the foundations of which were excavated in 1981. During those excavations only a part of a single pier was found, some 7m (23ft) east–west by 5m ($16\frac{1}{2}$ft) north–south, surviving to a height of 2.2m (7ft). However, this was sufficient to enable a scale model of the bridge to be built for the display in the Museum of London Roman gallery (**70** and **colour plate** 5). It shows a pier-based bridge built entirely of squared timbers rather than stone. The principles involved in this exercise differed somewhat from those already described in the two previous examples, but were based on the position and height of the timber pier as found, together with an understanding of what techniques the Roman engineers could be assumed to be familiar with, and the range of timber which they would have had at their disposal. Since the surviving pier (or main support) was of timber, it seemed reasonable to suggest that the rest of the superstructure would have been continued in that medium. It is clear

70 *The late first-century wooden bridge, as depicted in the model in the Museum of London* (Museum of London).

from excavations all along the London waterfront that all the Roman quay structures were built in timber, and so the necessary engineering experience was not lacking. Study of these waterfront structures shows that they were familiar with a range of lap joints, had the necessary expertise to shape and hoist large squared baulks into position, and were able to draw upon seemingly unlimited supplies of suitable oak. A Roman timber bridge could therefore be acceptable in principle, but its precise form required further research.

However, it is just as important to know about the river to be crossed as about the technical ex-

pertise of the engineers. Research in 1981–2 had shown that the first-century Thames was tidal but that the mean high-water mark was considerably lower than the levels attained by today's river. It was also over 300m wide at its narrowest point in the City reach in the Roman period, whereas the width of the embanked channel today in this area is between 200 and 250m.

Julius Caesar is known to have overseen the construction of a wooden bridge over the Rhine, but this seems to have been based on a series of vertically-driven piled trestles, rather than piers. Piers such as those recorded in London would be impractical for the non-tidal reach of a river, since it would only be possible to erect the horizontally-laid members on a foreshore exposed between tides. The technique could not be used in midstream. A possible solution which has been suggested might have involved the floating of piers into deep-water channel and then infilling them with rubble to sink them. However, such a technique, while appropriate for a continuous structure such as a breakwater, would not seem to offer much in the way of a guaranteed level or accurate position for piers laid out in that way. An alternative suggestion is that the bridge may well have changed to a piled substructure in midstream, a tried and tested bridge-building technique.

Thus it is argued that the foundations of our bridge may have used a combination of piles and piers to carry the decking; reflecting the tidal nature of the Thames. The piers must have been some 6–7m (20–23ft) apart, to allow for the passage of contemporary river craft. The beams supporting the decking must therefore have spanned such a distance without central support. It was therefore suggested that a cantilever system may have been used in which horizontally-laid timbers were stacked one upon the other, but with their ends jutting out and overlapping each other in a stepped formation. This solution most readily fits the evidence to hand, since it requires the same expertise and size of timbers as were already used in the foundation pier itself. All the necessary technology was unquestionably to hand.

The decking cannot have been much below c. +5m (16½ft) OD if it was intended that vessels would be able to pass beneath it at high tide. Alternatively, there may have been a movable drawbridge section, as there was in the late-medieval London Bridge from at least 1388 to 1722. The carriageway itself may well have been formed with a corduroy bed of logs over which clay and gravel was packed, a technique used to build Roman roads over unstable marshy ground. The suspended roadway was probably only 4 or 5m (13–16ft) wide, since the piers themselves were no more than 7m (23ft) across. This is substantially narrower than the 6–9m (20–30ft) widths recorded for the road approaching the bridge on both the northern and the southern sides, and suggests that the bridge would only have accommodated traffic moving in one direction at a time. This implies that access to it may have been strictly controlled at both ends. It is difficult to calculate the full length of this bridge since the line of the contemporary river bank on the Southwark shore has been destroyed by erosion. There may have also have been additional islands in midstream which the line of the crossing may have utilised. However, the mid-point of the bridge may have been marked by a shrine, since a remarkable concentration of coins was recovered from the bed of the Thames in the 1830s at that point, perhaps representing generations of offerings thrown into Old Father Thames to commemorate a safe passage. The coin concentration lay 160m south of the first-century City abutment. Given that the shrine was indeed in the middle of the span, then the bridge would have been some 320m long.

Roman replica boat

In September 1991 a new museum of waterfront archaeology opened at the Tower Hill Pageant in London. In the gallery is a full-sized section of a Roman quay, next to which is a much-decayed fragment of a Roman barge, discovered at Blackfriars in 1962–3. During the design stage, it was felt that such a fragment was a poor representative of Roman ship-building expertise, and so it was decided to build a full-sized replica of part of that boat to stand alongside the genuine quay timbers. This proved a most instructive exercise, for it was built largely using the same methods as the Romans probably used. In this way, the new museum obtained a splendid exhibit, the visitors were able to appreciate the size of the craft which once worked the River Thames, and we learned much about the problems and practicalities of Roman ship-building (**71**).

The wreck itself was recorded in difficult conditions during the rebuilding of the Thames embankment 30 years ago. It was a relatively flat-bottomed vessel some 16m (52ft) long and

71 *Damian Goodburn builds a replica of the Roman barge found at Blackfriars in 1962–3* (Museum of London).

just over 6m (20ft) wide, which had been built in *c.* AD 140, but sank later that century while carrying a cargo of building stone. Parts of what is thought to be the bow (the front end) and the port (left) side were recorded in detail, together with the mast-step, a large hewn timber spanning the bottom of the vessel with a squared hole cut in it in which the base of the mast would have been set. The mast itself would not have stood in the middle of the vessel, but was set approximately 5m (16½ft) away from the bow. The strength members of the boat comprised a series of closely-spaced ribs (floors) on the bottom of the craft, with additional members (futtocks) rising up the side. These were attached with iron spikes over 0.6m (2ft) long to the planks laid edge to edge which formed the shell of the boat. Each spike had been driven through the planks and frames, and then turned over on itself. This technique of ship building used in the northern part of the Roman empire was very different from the most common system found in the Medi-terranean region at this time. There the planking was joined edge to edge by means of a series of small tenons pegged into mortises; the wrecks on display at the Ship Museum in Ostia, near Rome were all built in that fashion, for example.

The reconstruction of the London ship was a difficult if rewarding task, supervised by Damian Goodburn, the Museum of London's Ancient Woodwork specialist. He studied the plans drawn during the original excavation of the wreck and prepared detailed scale-drawings from which he calculated the number and size of the planks and other timbers needed. The timber was provided by a co-operative forester, James Norman, who managed several large woods in Bromley, Kent, in which a number of oak trees had been blown down during the hurricane of October 1987. Many of the planks were sawn up into 5m (16½ft) lengths from logs in the woods using a trestle and a large two-man saw, in the way the Romans would have done it. This method leaves characteristic diagonal marks on the wood, and these have been identified on waterlogged Roman timber in third-century structures excavated on the amphitheatre site in London.

For the curved mast-step, futtocks and floor timbers, Damian selected as the original builders had done those parts of trees which had the appropriate naturally-grown shape, since this provides a much stronger element than cutting a straight timber into a curved shape. For example, the mast-step required a wide, thick timber 5m (16½ft) long, but one which curved up at both ends. The solution was to cut it from a tree which had a branch curving out at one end and a suitably-placed root at the other. Having cut the majority of the timbers to length, they were then transported (in a modern van) to the designated ship-building yard, a small park outside the Museum of London. Here, in full view of the general public, the construction of the Roman boat section took place, recreating a scene that would have been familiar to the inhabitants of Londinium 2000 years ago.

First, a raised platform of timber baulks was prepared upon which the boat could be built above the ground, so that we could crawl underneath the hull to gain access to the underside of the vessel. Then the timbers were cut to the specific shapes specified on the drawings, so that all the members fitted closely together. The edges of the planks had to be cut so that they bevelled and tapered, for example, which was done using the trestle and two-man saw as well as adzes and axes. The other members were carefully adzed to shape, and then the spike holes were marked up and drilled with an auger. However, the iron spikes could not be used at this stage, and so, as a temporary measure, the boat was held together with bolts. The timbers were liberally coated with vegetable oil to ensure that they did not dry out and crack too much.

The work progressed over the winter of 1990–1, and actually finished on time. No sooner had the boat been assembled than it had to be taken apart, for all the dressed component parts had to be fumigated to ensure that they carried no wood worm. Then they were transported to the new museum site at Tower Hill, and lowered one by one down the lift shaft into the gallery. Once all the numbered pieces had been brought together, the ship was reassembled for the final time, this time using the specially-manufactured iron spikes to bind the planks to the floors and futtocks. Next to our replica, the conserved section of a real Roman quay was laid, thus recreating a slice through the port of Roman London.

London archaeologists have used many methods to try and tell the story of Londinium in museum displays or in published reports. Each provides different levels of information for the visitor or reader, but each exercize also teaches the archaeologist different things about Roman life. We certainly learned more about Roman ship-building by actually trying to construct the boat than we ever could have by just reading about it. We learned about the tool kit they needed, and how best to use it. In addition, we learned something about the type and shape of trees that must have been common in the second-century woodland, fields and hedgerows when the original vessel was built. We were also able to reinterpret some aspects of the excavation records in the light of our experience, as we increased our understanding of the processes involved. Such projects are at least as valuable for the archaeologists undertaking them as for the public who see the final product or its accompanying video.

10

All creatures great and small

Over the last 20 years, archaeologists working on Roman sites in London have routinely recovered substantial quantities of pottery and other artefacts, the study of which has greatly assisted our understanding of the development of the town, its trading links, changes in technology, fashion and prosperity. The general approaches and methodologies concerned with such research are relatively well tried and tested. Indeed, as long ago as 1859, Charles Roach Smith was able to paint a remarkably detailed picture of Roman London by his careful cataloguing and study of finds collected from building sites. More recently, DUA specialists have produced important papers on a range of subjects, from pottery found in London, imported marbles to leather shoes. What is less well-known is the information which could be gained from the equally detailed research of the equally large assemblage of bones collected by the DUA from its London excavations. Such studies were not attempted for the sites investigated by the RMLEC or the Guildhall Museum, since the relevant resources were not made available, neither were the appropriate collection policies in place (**72**). This chapter will consider some of the avenues this line of research follows, by considering evidence for the range of creatures represented in the archaeological record; what they can tell us about the contemporary environment, the diet of the Roman Londoner, and ritual and religious practice.

The fauna of Londinium

The list of animals, birds and fish represented in the archaeological record for Roman London is gradually increasing, and does contain some surprises. Our evidence incorporates food debris discarded in pits, objects made from bone or antler and the debris associated with those handicrafts, the skeletons of creatures which had fallen into wells, carcasses which had been buried, and ritual deposits which had been interred for religious reasons.

In addition to cattle, pig and sheep (the principal components of the urban diet), the range of mammals identified includes hare, red deer, roe deer and, from a second-century deposit on the

72 *On some recent sites, a complex wet-sieving programme was introduced to ensure that small bones, such as those of birds and fish, were recovered* (Museum of London).

Watling Court site, evidence for a female fallow deer, the earliest evidence yet found in Britain for this species. The rural aspect of the Roman town is confirmed by the remains of mole, water vole, field vole, field mouse and common shrew. Animals which lived or worked alongside the human inhabitants of the town ranged from house mouse and black rat to horse, mule and dog; the carcasses of no fewer than nine dogs had been discarded in the base of an interval tower on the town wall, for example, while the evidence for several 'lap dogs', possibly pets, which were buried with more ceremony will be discussed later. A dog mandible recovered from the site at West Tenter Street is of especial interest since there were cut marks on it which have been identified as evidence of defleshing: this suggests the dog meat may have formed part of the late-Roman diet. The skeleton of a horse, recovered from the Miles Lane site, was about eight years old and had fused lumbar vertebrae, showing that it was probably used to haul heavy loads; and examination of the jaw bone of a mule from a waterfront site near Billingsgate showed that the creature had suffered rough treatment during its working life. Pack animals, either horses or mules, were also represented by the hoof-prints found in the mud beneath a Roman road next the Basilica site at Leadenhall Court. They were used to deliver to the site building materials, such as stone, off-loaded at the Thames quayside. The presence of these creatures was also marked on that building site by the charred remains of the hay and cereals which had formed their fodder.

Substantial evidence for domestic fowl, domestic duck and goose has been recovered, suggesting that such creatures were a familiar sight in the backyards of the Roman town. Common birds such as the starling and the song thrush are also represented. Taking a slightly wider view, the presence of the Thames is suggested by bones of night heron, grey heron, crane and mute swan, while a whole range of species conjures up a picture of the countryside beyond the town boundary as a mixture of

73 *Archaeological evidence recovered in 1986 on the site of the Basilica showed that a barn owl was roosting in the roof of the most prestigious building in Roman London. This modern barn owl, like its second-century predecessor, has captured a field vole* (photo by Robert T. Smith).

fields, woodland and pasture. The list is as impressive as it is evocative: woodcock, wood pigeon, dove, barn owl (**73**), raven, lapwing, golden plover and red kite, not to mention a white-tailed sea eagle. However, it should be stressed that birds such as the raven and the kite may have been equally at home scavenging in the city streets as in the open country.

Fish bones are small and are thus usually recovered by sieving soil samples. Since these techniques were developed relatively recently, most of the evidence for fish in Roman London has been collected since 1974. The freshwater species represented so far include eel, pike, cyprinid, dace, roach, gudgeon and chub, which suggest that the Thames and its tributaries provided a useful larder. However, the North Sea and the Channel were also exploited, since marine species such as sprat, smelt, cod, mackerel, haddock, and herring, were also found. There was also evidence for a Roman fish processing factory near Billingsgate. Within a building containing a timber-lined drain connected to a large sub-surface tank was a broken amphora in which whitebait, 84% herring and 16% sprat, were being converted into a fish sauce such as *garum* or *hallec*. The catch clearly came from local waters and provides further evidence of the Romano-British fishing industry. Huge dumps of oyster shells have also been found on the London waterfront, some as much as 2m (6½ft) deep, as at Regis House. Of the two large groups from the Pudding Lane site, one was first, the other second century in date, and their comparison proved constructive. Study of the particular organisms which had infested them suggested the oysters had been collected from the Kent or Essex coast. Significantly, it shows that the early group had been harvested from natural beds, whereas the second-century group with its larger, less distorted shells had come from new, artificial beds introduced by the Romans.

Environmental indicators

Since animals of all sizes often have a marked preference for a particular habitat, a record of their presence can reveal much about the contemporary environment. There must have been many animals which would have lived in Roman London alongside the human inhabitants but they may not have been a major component of the food resource and thus are not represented in the debris found in rubbish pits and midden deposits. Nevertheless, curious creatures often fell down wells or into pits and ditches, and are thereby preserved in the archaeological record. It is these unfortunate animals which provide an indication of the general conditions of the settlement, studies which can be supplemented by examination of the associated botanical evidence of seeds, pollen and so forth. For example, a late-Roman well from the Newgate Street site contained the bones of frog as well as the almost complete skeleton of a grass snake. Again, a

third-century well at 5 Fenchurch Street produced the skeletal remains of a juvenile, a sub-adult and one adult black rat. They were found together with the remains of several house mice. The site lies in the heart of the settlement next to the forum, in an area where occupation was intensive and where granaries and food stores flanked the busy market sector. This clearly represented an ideal environment for these rodents, but the infestation was not without risks to the townspeople, since the black rat is renowned as the host of the fleas which brought plague and pestilence with them. This is not the only context in which these unwelcome creatures have been found, for black rat, field mouse and house mouse were also recovered from the fourth-century ditch fills on the eastern side of the City at Crosswall. In addition, this ditch contained the limb bones and teeth of water vole, field vole and common shrew, as well as evidence of frog and grass snake. Taken together this produces a remarkably mixed rural and urban assemblage, showing how abruptly the town gave way to the country once one passed beyond the city ditch.

Another example of how the physical context of the town can be recreated through study of the bone evidence has recently been published, and was notable for adding another bird to our London list even though no avian bones were discovered in the sample. The deposit in question came from the heart of the Roman basilica itself, in a second-century level, where a pellet regurgitated by a barn owl was identified. It contained the remains of a mole and three voles, all creatures of rough grassland, and presumably was the product of a single night's work. Given that barn owls conduct the bulk of their hunting within a few hundred metres of the nesting site or roost, it therefore follows that substantial areas of pasture or rough grazing lay within easy reach of the civic centre, perhaps even within the town boundary.

Meat and butchery

Food refuse collected from pits, ditches and on

the floors of domestic buildings can provide insight into the diet and preferences of the Londoners. While of considerable interest in its own right, it is also important that the patterns noted in the City are compared with those on other contemporary urban, rural and military sites. A recent survey has suggested that a greater proportion of pork was eaten in villas than elsewhere, while the army ate more chicken than town dwellers, for example. That the evidence from London needs to be checked against the national picture is no less true for the faunal material than it is for ceramics, buildings and much else besides.

Recent research on a number of sites in Greater London showed that beef was the most popular meat, since ox bones were the most common find. Pork was the second most common item, and mutton a poor third. It has been suggested that bacon and lard were an important part of the Roman military diet, a preference apparently shared by the inhabitants of Londinium, at least in the early phase of occupation. The picture gained from study of the faunal remains from the settlement on the south bank produced a slightly different order, with beef first, then mutton followed closely by pork. Samples from elsewhere in Greater London show that pork was even less popular there. The significance of this lies in the suggestion by Dr Anthony King that one of the characteristics of Roman and 'Romanised' settlement was that they have a higher proportion of pig rather than sheep bones, while the reverse is true of a 'native celtic' site, where mutton was preferred.

That the proportion of cattle consumed compared with pig and sheep also seems to change over time has been shown by a major study of 1.1 metric tonnes of animal bone from 26 sites in the City: this suggests that cattle formed 77% of the total assemblage for the period AD 50–150, but that this rose to as much as 95% over the next one hundred years, dropping slightly to 90% from AD 250 to 400. Such apparent preferences may be reflecting food distribution systems as much as social class or ethnic mix, and clearly

more work needs to be done to identify the reasons for these most interesting variations.

Although bones of red deer, roe deer and hare have been found on a number of sites, there is little evidence to suggest that wild game animals were ever a major component of the diet in Roman London, north or south of the Thames.

Not all groups of faunal remains recovered from excavations represent the direct evidence of food consumed on the site. For example, the high proportion of lamb skull fragments from an early Roman ditch found on the 201 Borough High Street site in Southwark might indicate that the animals had been slaughtered and decapitated nearby, perhaps on a commercial scale, before the carcasses were sent elsewhere. Again, an early second-century pit on the Sir John Cass School site is thought to have contained the waste from a butcher's shop, since the majority of the bones were from the skull or feet of cattle, the bones which a butcher traditionally removes first while preparing the carcass for disjointing. London also had a thriving leather industry, perhaps based initially on military contracts, which seems to have been centred in the Walbrook area; part of a hide was found still staked out on Bucklersbury House excavation, while evidence for tanning was noted on a nearby site when the presence of latrine flies was identified (since urine was widely used in that process). It would not be unreasonable to suggest that the cattle were therefore slaughtered close by. Study of the London material is therefore proving of great interest, and will continue to do so since the bone recovered from City excavations comprises one of the largest stratified groups of such data in the whole country.

Bone-working

Animal bone and antler were used in the manufacture of a wide range of items in Londinium, as examples of the finished product and detritus of the manufacturing process prove. How-ever, not all the items need to have been actually made in the town from local products, as the discovery of an imported comb made from elephant ivory shows. Nevertheless, clear evi-dence of bone and antler working has been recovered from Roman refuse deposits on the St Swithin's House and Bank of England sites in the Walbrook valley, for example. Here the sawn red-deer foot (metatarsal) bones and fragments of deer antlers presumably represent the debris left over from the manufacture of knife handles, while the sawn sections of ox metatarsals may be the waste from the manufacture of lathe-turned hinges or cylinders. On the Copthall Avenue site, also in the semi-industrial zone of the Walbrook valley, triangular bone-weaving tablets were being sawn out of the shoulder blades (scapulae) of cattle. The evidence comes from a study of 29 such scapulae from adult cattle, from different contexts and from which some 90 triangular pieces had been sawn. The activity was clearly being conducted on the site, since two of the finished, if damaged, triangular weaving tablets were also found, the first time that both the waste and the final product of this process have been identified together. It was on this same site, incidentally, that horse and cattle bone waste proved to be an environmental indicator. Study of these bones showed deep scoring and scuff marks. This was not evidence of bone-working, but showed that they had been subjected to considerable wear from the passing of hob-nailed boots. It seems that bones had been laid over boggy ground to provide a dry surface.

Ritual burial

There are many examples of burials found in Roman London which relate to rituals or religious practices, the reasons for which have all but eluded us. What, for instance, might be the significance of the pit excavated at the first-and second-century cemetery in Clare Street, in which was found two broken flagons sealing the complete skeleton of a heron, together with the remains of several shrews, some voles and 80 frogs? The late Dr Ralph Merrifield made a detailed study of such fascinating deposits. He has shown that foundation offerings, or the rite of commencement, are known from many

Roman sites, usually in the form of animal or bird sacrifice, or with pots containing food or drink. A young lamb was found sealed beneath a first-century wall on the Leadenhall Court site, while a small dog had been interred below a second-century wall on the Newgate Street site (**74**). Since in both cases the buildings had been rebuilt after fire damage, perhaps the deposits were to prevent a reoccurrence of such events.

Human skeletal studies

Enigmatic ritual practices have also been suggested as the explanation for the discovery of human skulls from the upper Walbrook valley; since the early nineteenth century (if not earlier) hundreds have been found during development of the area around Moorgate. Of these some 50 sur-vive today in museum collections in London and Oxford. More recently, other examples have been recovered from controlled excavations at Copthall Avenue and 52 London Wall. These macabre discoveries were once thought to represent the victims of the Boudican revolt in AD 61. However, studies have subsequently suggested that they are more likely to be the consequence of celtic ritual practices, in which the heads of

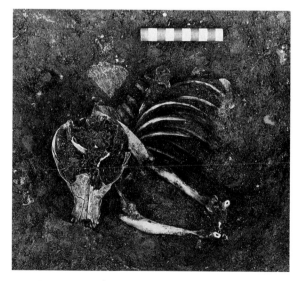

74 *A dead dog. This small dog was deliberately buried beneath a second-century building on the Newgate Street site, perhaps to placate the gods and bring the prospective occupants good luck* (Museum of London).

deceased persons were deposited into the sacred river Walbrook as part of religious rite. It is possible that a shrine or sacred precinct of undetermined type may have marked the place at which the rituals were conducted. Since the practice seems to have continued into the early Roman period, the skulls bear witness to the presence of Britons who may have tolerated and even benefited from Romanisation, but whose underlying philosophy remained celtic to the very bitter end. The cult may be associated in some way with the discovery of the severed head of a bronze statue of the emperor Hadrian, which was found deposited in the Thames in 1834.

To turn to the human remains recovered from the official late-Roman cemeteries just beyond the town wall: the study of this material will be able to say much about the citizens themselves as well as about their religious practices (**75**). Substantial groups of burials have been recorded from these sites. Since 1983, for example, there have been nine excavations and numerous observations conducted by the Department of Greater London Archaeology in the extensive cemetery to the east of the City: over 104 cremations and 575 inhumations were recorded in this period. The range of information which such studies will provide can be seen from the work undertaken on the large group of burials from part of the West Tenter Street site, which forms part of this eastern cemetery. The report gives details on 120 inhumations from the large second-to-fourth-century cemetery there. For example, the mean height of male skeletons was 1.71m (about 5ft 7in), based on a sample of 44 measurable skeletons, whereas for females it was 1.57m (about 5ft 2in), although the sample here was only 15. It seems that the lead level in many of the bones was higher than would be expected today, a finding supported by work on cemeteries elsewhere in Britain. Drinking water from lead pipes, the preparation or consumption of food and drink in lead or pewter vessels could be contributory factors. Three cases of Diffuse Idiopathic Skeletal Hyperostosis (DISH) were also identified, of which all were relatively

75 *Roman Londoner: a former citizen of Londinium uncovered in 1989, on the cemetery site in West Smithfield* (Museum of London).

young: one was under 40, the other two not much older. This particular disease is a degenerative disorder which occurs in some 3% of the modern population. However, DISH is almost never diagnosed in living patients before the age of 40. As a consequence, the study of the disease today is limited to its later stages, since it cannot be identified until the patient has complained. Palaeo-pathologists are therefore in the privileged position of being able to observe skeletal change at whatever stage the disease happens to be at time of death. As Dr Tony Waldron observes, they are therefore able to contribute to the knowledge of such diseases; a fine example of the maxim which used to adorn the entrance to the autopsy room: *Mortui viventes docent*, 'The dead teach the living'.

Over 127 inhumations were recorded at the Giltspur Street site in 1989 (**76**) to add to the 20

76 *A cemetery under excavation: digging, cleaning and planning at Giltspur Street in 1989* (Museum of London).

examined earlier on the neighbouring St Bartholomew Hospital site, both on the north-west side of the town. This cemetery extended at least as far west as Barnard's Inn, Holborn, since three burials and two cremations were excavated there in 1988. To the north of the City, over 70 burials have been recorded since 1986 on sites on both sides of Ermine Street, which broadly follows the line of Bishopsgate, while a further 12 inhumations have recently been recovered from the cemetery around Moorgate. Taken together this forms a sample from sites on the north bank of over 220 burials which have yet to be analysed, while the cemeteries from Southwark provide yet more data.

The next stage must be to provide a larger data base of information from London on age at death, cause of death, average height, chronic disorders and so forth, after which comparative work can be undertaken on groups from other Roman settlements in Britain and elsewhere. After that, comparisons can be made with the large groups of Saxon, later medieval and post-medieval burials recovered form the City. We may then be able to suggest whether or not Londinium was a healthier place in which to live than was its Saxon successor.

The conclusion of our summary study of the bones retrieved from 20 years of excavation in London can only serve to highlight the considerable potential of this material; much remains to be done. The work can really only begin after the excavators have assessed the field records and provided firm, dated phasing for the assemblages, a continuing process.

As a postscript, mention must be made of the ox tibia found in Roman levels from the Tower of London: it had an iron *ballista* (catapult) bolt shot through it. The picture which that single bone creates neatly encapsulates a moment in the life of late-Roman London, for it shows how troops manning the artillery mounted on the defences, engaged in target practice on live animals grazing in open pasture outside the walls. The bones from Londinium have as important a tale to tell as any inscription.

11

Citizens

This book is unashamedly based on the physical, archaeological evidence for Londinium rather than on the written or historical sources, for the reasons presented in Chapter 1. However, there is fascinating body of data which cannot be overlooked and which can lay claim to be both archaeological and historical. Inscriptions, whether on tombstones, writing tablets, or ead plaques, as graffiti scratched on pottery or on walls, or as names stamped on knives or ingots, all speak eloquently about those who once lived and worked in Roman London. A wide range of such evidence has been collected by the many individuals and organisations who have struggl-ed to record the archaeology of the City over the last three centuries or so. The Museum of London has in its galleries, for example one tombstone dis-covered in 1669, in the very first decades of serious archaeological research in the City. By 1928, a list had been compiled which contained 110 London inscriptions, although this included some very fragmentary examples. Since then, more have been recovered during work in and around the City, most notably the important group of ins-cribed stones reused in a late Roman defensive work on the Baynard's Castle site and the marble plaque discovered in Southwark in 1984.

Unfortunately there are very few inscriptions which help the archaeologist date and identify the major buildings in the town. True, there are references to particular temples, or at least to the gods to whom shrines were dedicated, carved on altars to Mithras, Jupiter and Isis, for example. There is also the famous flagon from Southwark upon which is scratched the legend LONDINI AD FANUM ISIDIS, 'at London, at the temple of Isis'. It is also possible that a temple dedicated to the deified Emperor was established in London, if the reading of a fragmentary inscription, NUM C...PROV... BRITA (NUM*ini Caesaris*... PROV*incia*... BRITA*nnia*) is accepted as: 'to the deity of the Emperor, the Province of Britain set this up'. However, we have yet to find the inscriptions to date the building of the basilica or identify precisely where the Governor's residence was. The closest we have come to such a discovery was at the Huggin Hill bath-house in 1989, where Purbeck marble fragments possibly from a single dedicatory inscription were recovered, including the letters MAX ... NIA and AUG.

This chapter summarises some of the personal names and occupations recorded in inscriptions from Londinium. It can do no more than provide a flavour of the rich vein of research which these studies represent. Taken together, the names provide a vivid insight into the lives and languages of Londinium and complement an otherwise impersonal sequence of building plans. Our inscriptions show that the town's population would have been very mixed. For some of its history, the provincial Governor lived here, together with his staff and associated military detachments, but there were also craftsmen, work-men, merchants, retired soldiers, freedmen, slaves, men, women and children. The inscriptions demonstrate that Latin was spoken, written and read, however badly; some of the Latin used on the Metunus curse is notably vernacular in style and ungrammatical in form, for example. Personal names such as 'Olussa' and 'Hector', and funerary monuments with Greek inscriptions show that Greek was also known here. Other provinces represented in the city include Gaul and Asia Minor. Unfortunately the Celtic languages spoken by the native Britons are not well represented in the written record. However, 'Thames' and 'London' are both based on Celtic words and there are some British personal names, such as 'Dagobitus'. The alter gave his daughter the Latin name of 'Grata'; a sign of the increasing Romanization of the indigenous population. All in all, Londinium seems to have been a cosmopolitan city, struggling with an unfamiliar language in its eagerness to adopt the trappings of Romanisation.

Officials

It would seem appropriate to begin the list with evidence of the Imperial Legate, the provincial Governor himself, since by the end of the first century the Governor and his staff would have been based here. A third-century inscription discovered in 1975 (**77**) made reference to the hitherto unknown Governor who oversaw the restoration of a temple, one M. Martiannius Pulcher.

The official in charge of the finances of the province, the Procurator, would also have been based in Londinium. Parts of a tombstone, discovered in 1852 and 1935, commemorate Julius Alpinus Classicianus, the Procurator responsible for reorganising the province after the Boudican revolt. The presence of this tombstone suggests that, since he seems to have died in Londinium, this Procurator may have been living and working there in AD 61. Other evidence of the Procurator's presence has been recovered in the form of bricks with the official stamp PP BR LON (*Procurator Provinciae Britanniae Londinii*) which have been recovered from sites in the City, Southwark and Westminster; writing

77 *This altar discovered reused in the riverside wall at Blackfriars in 1976 was from a temple which, the inscription informs us, was restored by M. Martiannius Pulcher. This gentlemen was probably the provincial Governor in AD 251–9 (Sue Hurman).*

tablets which had been branded as issued from his office; and an iron stamp M P BR (?*Metalla Provinciae Britanniae*) which probably refers to the mines of the province of Britain. A timber from the amphitheatre which is stamped MIBL and ICLV may also be connected with official supplies.

One of the inscribed altars discovered in 1975 on the Baynard's Castle site records the name of

Aquilinus, described as the 'emperor's freedman', the only such attribution yet known from London. The gentlemen must have been one of the trusted advisers in the imperial household. Three colleagues are also mentioned on the same stone, although no indication of their status is given: they are Mercator, Audax and Graecus; who may have also been engaged as officials of some sort in the Imperial service.

Military

There would have been a strong military presence in Roman London, since all the Legions serving in Britannia would have had detachments based there in the Cripplegate Fort. Writing tablets found in Vindolanda near Hadrian's Wall refer to a cohort of Tungrians sent to support the Governor in London in AD 90, and also to a letter from Chrauttius to Veldius, the Governor's groom in London. The military tombstones recovered to date record the names of sixteen soldiers serving with the Governor, including two centurions: (Sempro)nius Sempro(nianus) and Vivius Marcianus of *Legio II Augusta*. Another centurion's name is recorded on the head of a spear found in 1954 in a well containing late-first-century pottery. A translation of the inscription C VER VICT suggests that the spear belonged to the detachment commanded by Verus Victor. In 1950 the British Museum acquired a bronze legionary helmet which had been found in the Thames or Walbrook some years before. The punched graffiti on the neck-guard has given us no less than seven names of soldiers who may have served in Londinium. It seems that the helmet had at least four owners, who were: Lucius Dulcius in the century of Marcus Valerius Ursus; Rufus in the century of Scribonius; Lucius Postumus and Aulus Saufeius, both of whom were in the century of Martialis, though presumably not at the same time. In all, three of the six legions (*legio*) which served in Britannia are mentioned on London funerary monuments, of which *Legio II Augusta* is the most common. We have the names of several soldiers from

that legion: Celsus and his colleagues, also presumably from the same unit, Dardanius Cursor, Probus and Rubrius Pudens, as well as Ulpius Silvanus. Also recorded are Flavius Agricola from *Legio VI Victrix*, and Julius Valens, Gaius Acilius M(...) and probably Saturninus, all from *Legio XX Valeria Victrix*. A tombstone from Camomile Street, found in 1876, represented another military official, perhaps seconded to the Governor for special duties; while a more recently discoverd tombstone from Winchester Palace in Southwark (**78**) lists seven soldiers who may also have served a similar role, although only the names of three are readable: Severus, Martinus and a Germanic-sounding Gontius. This is by no means the only military find from Southwark: a military lead tag found on the Courage Brewery site in 1984 had a cursive inscription which refers to a century led by Cornelius Verecundus.

There is also some evidence that another military unit was represented in London: the *Classis Britannica*. This was the fleet which was raised to transport the Roman army to Britain in AD 43, and which then provided support for all subsequent military operations there. Although the principal base of the fleet in Britain is known to have been at Dover, at least from *c*. AD 130 to 200, there is every reason to suppose that there was an office in Londinium attached to the Governor's staff. There were, for example, substantial detachments of the Misene and Ravenna fleets at Rome (far from their bases in the Bay of Naples and the Adriatic), keeping in close contact with the imperial administration there. Tiles stamped with the legend CL BR (*Classis Britannica*) have been found in England, all from sites between London, Richborough and Pevensey, but most commonly from Beauport Park and Dover. In addition to a substantial number of unstamped tiles with the same fabric as the CL BR tiles from sites in the City and Southwark, (from the Winchester Palace, Calvert's Building and Cotton's Wharf sites), there are now three stamped tiles from Londinium, one of which shares the same stamp die as one from Dover

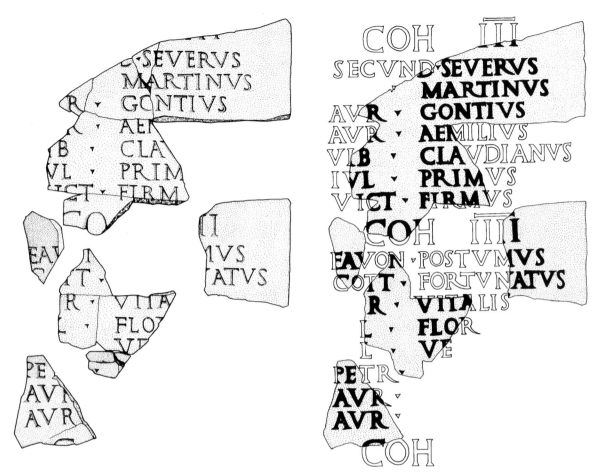

78 *Fragments of a marble inscription discovered on the Winchester Palace site, Southwark in 1988. It records the names of soldiers, listed by cohort, who were seconded to serve the governor in Londinium. (Left) the fragments as found; (right) a reconstruction of part of the list (Sue Hurman).*

dated to 190–210. Another find which may perhaps be associated with the presence of a detachment of the *Classis Britannica* is the miniature bronze prow of a warship found in London in 1850, and now in the British Museum. It is inscribed with neat letters written backwards, suggesting that it was a votive object laid in a shrine to celebrate a naval victory or to pray for help in a battle to come. It reads *Ammilla Aug Felix*, which could be translated as 'be lucky Ammilla, warship of our Emperor'.

Apart from serving soldiers, London no doubt also had its share of veterans living there. A fragment of a bronze military diploma which conferred citizenship on the recipient, was re-covered from a second-century, fire-damaged building on the Watling Court site in 1978. Unfortunately the name of the veteran who had served in the army for 25 years did not survive, but the name of a witness, Quintus Pompeius Homerus, did.

Craftsmen

Moneyers are represented by the mint marks on the coins from the short-lived London mint which was in operation *c.* 290–326 and again briefly in the 380s, but it seems unlikely that there were more than five or six moneyers working there. Initially, the mint marks were L (*Londinii*); ML (*moneta Londinii*) and SML (*sacra moneta Londinii*) but these were changed after 296 to LN or LON (*Londinii*) and PLN (*percussa Londinii*) 'struck in London'. The marks after 305 also included PLON and PL (*percussa Londinii*), MLL (*moneta L? Londinii*) and MLN (*moneta Londinii*). A silver ingot found in 1777 in the Tower of London with coins of Honorius (395–423) and Arcadius (395–408) was stamped with the mark EX OFFE HONORINI (from the workshop of Honorinus)

The names of craftsmen, some of whom presumably plied their trade in Londinium, have been found stamped on several items. Most notably, this group includes four knives with *P Basili f(ecit)* or a similar legend. This has been interpreted as: 'P (...), the slave of Basilius, made this.' If this reading is correct, it seems to show that London patrons were setting up slaves or freedman in business.

Since the rest of the names inscribed on the items in this group appear but once, they are, therefore, less certainly local craftsmen. The list includes a chisel *Aprilis*; a bone comb *Dignus*; a bone scraper *Ceres Equitis* (perhaps 'wax of Eques'?); a razor *Germanu*; a bronze bell *Martinus*, and two examples stamped on the handle of a bronze patera, *T Rufus C* and *Sangus*. A samian vessel had *L Jul Senis crocod ad aspr* stamped upon it, which is thought to refer to 'Julius Senis's ointment for roughness [of the eyes]', and therefore represents an occultists stamp used for impressing the message on cakes of ointment.

There is also evidence for heavy industries, with a reference to the building of ships, in a writing tablet which mentions *navem faci...* as well as a steering oar *clavi faciendi*. Brick manufacture also produced inscriptions: *tegulae* found in Cloak Lane in 1989 bore the stamps of the kilns of *Decimus M... Val...* and *Decimus M... P*, for example. In addition to the officially stamped tiles already discussed, several have graffiti upon them. The most celebrated is the specimen with AUSTRALIS DIBUS XIII VAGATURSIB COTIDIM carved into the clay while still wet (i.e., before the tile was fired) and therefore written by a brickmaker who was clearly more or less literate and numerate. He was also somewhat aggrieved, since the inscription reads: 'Augustalis has been going off by himself every day for these thirteen days.'

Commerce

Evidence for commercial transactions comes from two main sources. The first includes inscriptions painted onto storage jars imported into Britannia, of which several have been found in London. Among the more legible examples is one on an amphora from Southwark which trans-lates as: 'Lucius Tettius Africanus' finest fish sauce from Antipolis'; one from the City which contained produce 'from the estate of Caius Acerronius Fur(...)'; and on an amphora neck which proclaimed its contents as '250 ... [?kilos] ... of green olives; transported by Gaius L(...) of Avernus'. Greek names have also been found on this imported pottery: the Koan amphora re-cently found on a London Wall site bore the Greek name Theourou while one from Huggin Hill was inscribed with a Greek version of Severus. Barrels were sometimes marked in a similar way: one found in 1914 had been stamped T C PACATI. All these names presumably represent foreign concerns with which Londinium did business. The recent discovery in West Smithfield of a wine amphora with a 25-litre capacity provides evidence of British trade, for it had been made in the kilns at Brockley Hill, to the north of London. It bore the stamp *Senecionus*, who may have been the potter or the owner of the native vineyard which was supplying Londinium with wine at that date.

Even more detailed evidence comes from writing tablets, such as one now in the British Museum but found in the Walbrook in 1927. The address on the outside reads *Londinio ... L Vita Ad s(...)*. The message within begins: *Rufus callisuni salutem epillico et omnibus contubernalibus...* 'Rufus, son of Callisunus: greetings to Epillicus and all his fellows.' It continues by requesting that a list be sent, that matters be looked after, and that: *illam puellam ad nummum redigas* ('the girl be turned into cash'). One translation of this phrase suggests that it may well refer to the slave trade. Another tablet discusses 'the money by the terms likewise of the claim shall be paid to me by Crescens or by the person concerned'. In 1986, another writing tablet was recovered from an excavation near the Walbrook. This one proved to be concerned with legal proceedings arising from a disputed property in what is now Kent; the gentlemen involved was called Lucius Iteius Betucus, a name which suggests he may have been an Italian.

Men

The names of several civilian men are commemorated by inscriptions on tombstones or, in one case, on a sarcophagus. Although the age at death was legible in only two instances, it was at least 70 years in both cases. The gentlemen in question were Flavius, who may have been from Antioch, and A. Alfidius Olussa, who was born in Athens. The others were M. Aurelius Eucarpus, G. Etruscus, T. Licinius Ascanius, Primus, and Valerius Amandinus, whose sarcophagus was prepared by his sons Valerius Marcellus and Valerius Superrentor. Other funerary inscriptions include that from the Hooper Street cemetery which recorded: 'Lucius Pompeius Licetus Da(...), from Arretium'.

A tombstone found on Ludgate Hill in 1806 records the name of Anencletus, described as a 'slave of the province' who seems to have been in the service of the Provincial Council, a body which represented all British tribes. He may have been involved in the organisation of the state cult of emperor worship, for which a major temple was presumably built in the city, perhaps represented by the NUM C... PROV... BRITA... inscription mentioned previously.

Graffiti on pottery and stones furnishes us with the following London names: Alexander, Audax, Candidus, Celer, Eques, Felicula, Felix, Gaius, Glycera, Julius, Julianus, Marus, Marcus, Optatus, Paulus, Petronius, Priscus, Restitua, Titullus, Turpillus (who wished drinkers from a wine jar good luck) and Verecundus. A leather off-cut and a shoe were incised with the names

Liber and Hector respectively, while T. Egnatius Tyrannus and Publius Cicereius Felix appear on a lead curse. Another such item, discovered near London Bridge in 1984, asked Metunus (Neptune) for vengeance within nine days on: Silviola, Sattavillus, son of Silvicola, Avitus, Santinus, Mag(...), (...)etus, (...)apidimis Antonius, Santus Vasianus and Varasius. A lead sealing from Billingsgate had once been owned by Marcus Maximus, *primus pilus*, as had been a finger-ring from the same site by Gaius Flavius, son of Gaius.

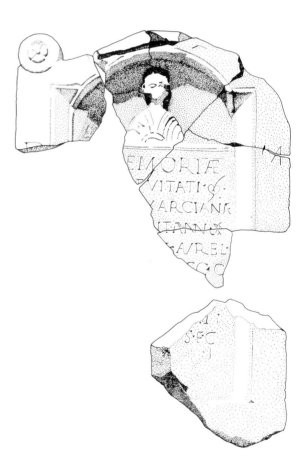

79 *The memorial to Marciana, who died, aged ten, in third-century Londinium. These fragments were broken up and used as hard core in the foundations of a fourth-century bastion built against the defensive wall at Crosswall, near Aldgate (Sue Hurman).*

Women

Funerary monuments are our principal source for female names from Londinium. Those represented include the wife of the Procurator Classicianus, Julia Pacata Indiana and Claudia Martina who died aged nineteen, and had been the wife of the Imperial slave Anencletus. Other names include Albia Faustina, Aurelia Eucarpia, Atia, Grata (who died aged 40), Januaria Martina and Tullia Numidia. The excavations at Crosswall in 1980 recovered a tombstone set up by Aurelius (presumably the grieving father) to commemorate a young girl, Marciana, who had died aged ten (**79**).

We know little else about most of these people beyond their names, but there are two other characters who merit mention, both immortalised on lead plaques as part of a curse. One was found in Union Street Southwark in 1989, and had *Martia Martina sive* (Martia a.k.a. Martina) inscribed upon it backwards. Why she was being cursed was not recorded. The other was one *Tretia* (probably a mistake for Tertia) *Maria* whose name also appears on a lead plaque as part of a curse. She had obviously upset someone, for the message reads: 'I curse Tretia Maria and her life and mind and memory and liver and lungs mixed up together and her words thoughts and memory. Thus may she be unable to speak what things are concealed nor be able…' Fortunately, the rest of the plaque is missing.

12

The remains of Roman London

Unlike Pompeii or Rome, there is little surviving above ground to remind the Londoner or the visitor of the City's Roman past. However, the broad contours of the ancient city can still be made out by those armed with imagination and disdain for London's traffic. The valley of the River Fleet lies at the foot of Ludgate Hill, and even the infilled Walbrook valley can be seen by those looking west along Cannon Street towards St Paul's. The steep slopes that ran down to the Thames remain, although the great river itself and the vessels which plied it are now represented by juggernauts lumbering along Upper and Lower Thames Street. As for upstanding remains, most of what is left is marked on fig. **80**. The town wall is by far the largest fragment, and a wall-walk was established in May 1984 when 21 explanatory plaques were set up. This walk traces the line of the City wall from just north of the Tower of London (1) to Alders-gate (21), near the Museum of London. There is also an impressive fragment of the riverside wall exposed within the precinct of the Tower of London (**front cover**), although this is not part of the official wall-walk (31). At Tower Hill (2), where the wall survives 4.4m (14½ft) high, there is a replica of the memorial plaque to Julius Classicianus, a provincial Procurator. The recent programme of excavations saw a further section of the wall preserved at Emperor House, Crosswall (4), although this is not always accessible. At Duke's Place (6) mosaic murals in an underpass mark the line of the wall and internal bank. Parts of both the town and the fort walls are visible in St Alphege gardens (12). The west gate to the Cripplegate Fort is locked up in a car park nearby (18), but is opened up to visitors on the first Tuesday (10.30 a.m. to 12 p.m.) and the third Friday (2.30 p.m. to 4 p.m.) in the month, not the most memorable of opening times. An impressive section of wall survives at the far end of the same underground carpark. The town wall, fort and internal turret foundations (19) are visible above ground in Noble Street, provided the undergrowth has been cleared.

A reconstituted Temple of Mithras (25), complete with crazy paving, has been laid out in the forecourt of Temple Court, 11 Queen Victoria Street, having been lifted from its original location on the east side of the Walbrook. Late Roman mosaic pavements and a range of artefacts collected during redevelop-ments on the site of the Bank of England are now displayed in a museum in the bank in Threadneedle Street: there is no admission charge, and it is open on weekdays from 10 a.m. to 5 p.m., and on Sundays from 11 a.m. to 5 p.m. in the summer (26). A commemorative plaque recording the site of the second-century basilica has been set up in the foyer of Marks and Spencer, at Leadenhall Court (27). Some fragments of that great building still survive *in situ* in basements but public access to them is, to say the least, limited: for example, part of a contemporary wall lies beneath 73 Cornhill and a pier is in 90

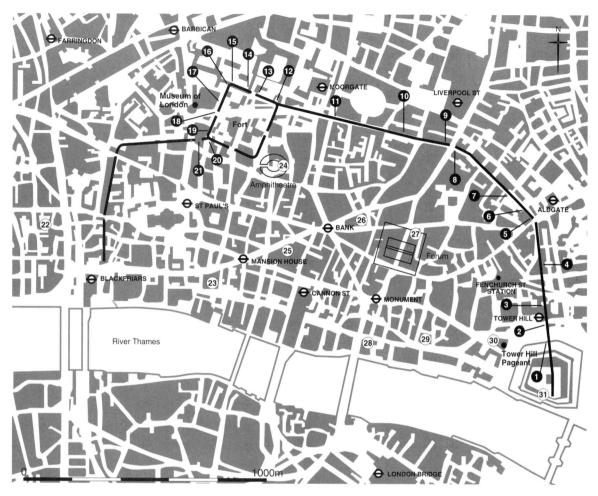

80 *This map shows the location of some surviving Roman features in relation to the modern street system in the City (Chrissie Milne).*

The numbers in the black circles represent plaques on the Wall Walk which describe fragments of the Roman and Medieval City defences. Numbers in white circles are:

22) St Bride's church, tessellated pavement
23) Dominant House: part of Huggin Hill bath-house hidden beneath the basement floor, safe but not on display. A fragment was visible in adjacent garden
24) Guildhall: when new Art Gallery is completed, part of the amphitheatre will be on display
25) Temple Court: Mithraeum replica (not in situ)
26) Bank of England Museum
27) Leadenhall Court: plaque marks site of basilica
28) St Magnus church: forlorn fragment of Roman quay
29) Lower Thames Street: bathhouse, not on public display
30) All Hallows church: Roman features in crypt

Gracechurch Street; neither of these monuments is on public display. As for other buildings, tessellated pavements are visible in the crypt of St Bride's church, Fleet Street (22) and in All Hallows by the Tower (30). Although half a bath-house lies under 100 Lower Thames Street (29) and half of another one lies under Senator House near Huggin Hill (23), neither is at present open to visitors; this may change in the future. The remains of the eastern entrance to the amphitheatre will, however, be visibly incorporated in the new development of the Guildhall art gallery (24). In the forecourt of St Magnus Church near London Bridge, open to the weather, is a forlorn baulk of timber from the first-century quay discovered on the Regis House site 60 years ago (28). The fact that it survives at all after 2000 years is remarkable; that nobody ever visits it even more so.

All in all, the sum total is not as dramatic as one might wish, but this is compensated for by some remarkable museum displays: the Roman gallery at the Museum of London (now being replanned), contained life-sized room reconstructions, models, a remarkable range of artefacts displayed thematically, funerary monuments, mosaic floors and wall paintings. In Bloomsbury, the British Museum houses part of the Charles Roach-Smith collection, much of which was collected in the City in the nineteenth century. In September 1991, the new Tower Hill Pageant was opened, which incorporates a gallery of material recently excavated from the London waterfront. It includes a section of Roman quay and a replica section of the Blackfriars ship, as well as pottery and other artefacts. Anyone interested in Roman London should try and visit all these museums.

Museum of London, London Wall, EC2
Tues–Sat 10 a.m. to 6 p.m.
Sun 2 p.m. to 6 p.m.; Mon closed
Admission charges

Tower Hill Pageant, Tower Hill, EC3
Mon–Sun 9.30 a.m. to 5.30 p.m. (summer)
9.30 a.m. to 4.30 p.m. (winter)
Admission charges

British Museum, Great Russell Street, WC1
Mon–Sat 10 a.m. to 5 p.m.
Sun 2.30 p.m. to 6 p.m
Admission free

Further reading

A library for Londinium

There is a feast of further reading available on Roman London ranging from attractive booklets to dense archive reports. In between are various books, monographs and articles in periodicals, since the DUA's work was published in a spread of journals and sundry other outlets, rather than in a single series of its own. Given the extensive and developing nature of the excavation programme between 1973 and 1991, it is important to appreciate how our knowledge developed: for example, prior to 1981 there was much speculation as to where the Roman bridge was; before 1988 the location of the amphitheatre was unknown. It is, therefore, of considerable importance to note the *date* of each publication, since each new year adds new discoveries which might overturn earlier ideas.

Introductory material

Particularly useful are those produced for the Museum of London, such as *The London Wall Walk* by H. Chapman et al., (1985); J. Hall & R. Merrifield's *Roman London* (1986), C. Jones' *Roman Mosaics* (1988), and the Ordnance Survey's map of Londinium (revised edition, 1983), although only a small proportion of the more recent finds are plotted on this sheet. The DUA's work is summarised in *Archaeology of the City of London* (1980); B. Hobley's *Roman & Saxon London: a reappraisal* (1986) and annual reports on work in the City between 1988 and 1989, edited by C. Spence and F. Grew (1989; 1990), while *MoLAS '94* is a general report covering the period 1992–3.

General books

For the work undertaken before the DUA began, a selection must include R. Merrifield's *The Roman City of London* (Benn, 1965); W. F. Grimes's *The Excavation of Roman & Medieval London* (Routledge 1968) and the survey by M. Biddle *The Future of London's Past* (Rescue, 1973). P. Marsden's *Roman London* (Thames & Hudson, 1980) contains studies of the Guildhall Museum's pre-1973 programme as well as some DUA material, as does Merrifield's *London, City of the Romans* (Batsford, 1983) but the most recent study is that by D. Perring, *Roman London* (Seaby, 1991). All these books have very useful bibliographies upon which further research can be planned. The best library for locating material is the Guildhall Library in Aldermanbury, EC2.

Special studies

These books or monographs include various areas of thematic studies such as those published by the *Council for British Archaeology* on particular zones of Roman London: e.g., C. Maloney, *The Upper Walbrook Valley* (no. 69, 1990); D. Perring & S. Roskams, *Development of Roman London west of the Walbrook*, (no. 70, 1990); T. Williams, *Public Buildings in the South-west Quarter of Roman London* (no. 88, 1993) and a long-awaited report on pottery by B. Davies (no. 5, 1995).

The CBA also published conference proceedings which included London material such as: J. Maloney & B. Hobley (eds), *Roman Urban Defences in the West* (no. 51, 1983) and F. Grew & B. Hobley (eds), *Roman Urban Topography in Britain and the Western Empire* (no. 59, 1985). Contact: Council for British Archaeology, Bowes Morrell House, 111 Walmgate, York, YO1 2UA.

Other detailed studies include two by P. Marsden, *Roman Forum Site in London* (HMSO, 1987) and *Ships of the Port of London* (English Heritage, 1994) and two by G. Milne, *The Port of Roman London* (Batsford 1985, reprinted 1993) and *From Roman Basilica to Medieval Market* (HMSO, 1992). Future publications include those being prepared for English Heritage by the Museum of London on the excavations conducted by Professor Grimes on the Mithraeum and Cripplegate Fort.

London & Middlesex Archaeological Society

This venerable body began publishing their annual transactions for subscribers in 1855 and is still going strong. The journal has carried many important articles, although you will have to consult it in a reference library unless you are a member of the Society. From 1976 it also produced a Special Paper series including a compilation of studies in J. Bird *et al.*, (eds) *Collectanae Londiniensia* (no. 2, 1978). Others in the series include: C. Hill *The Riverside Wall and Monumental Arch* (no. 3, 1980); D. Jones, *Excavations at Billingsgate Buildings*, 1974 (no. 4, 1980); J. M. C Toynbee *Roman Art Treasures from the Temple of Mithras* (no. 7, 1986); L. Miller *et al.*, *Roman Quay at St Magnus House* (no. 8, 1986); T. Wilmott *Excavations in the Middle Walbrook Valley* (no. 13, 1991). These reports all incorporate important finds studies.

Contact: London & Middlesex Archaeological Society, c/o Museum of London, London Wall, London EC2Y 5HN

Britannia

The Society for the Promotion of Roman Studies was founded in 1970 and produces a yearly periodical for subscribers and all good libraries called *Britannia*. It has frequently contained articles on London material, including studies of marble, wall plaster, coins from the Thames, leatherwork, writing tablets, the harbour and Basilica, as well as an annual round-up of work in Britain (including London) which incorporates notes on all inscriptions found that previous year. Contact: The Society for the Promotion of Roman Studies, c/o Institute of Archaeology, 31 Gordon Square, London WC1H OPY.

The London Archaeologist

This quarterly magazine was founded in 1968 and has subsequently carried a range of important interim reports on current projects on, for example, the amphitheatre site as well as on some old favourites. It also is contains a comprehensive summary of all fieldwork conducted in the London area in the previous year.

Contact: The London Archaeologist, 8 Woodview Crescent, Hildenborough, Tonbridge, Kent TN11 9HD.

Other periodicals

Reports on recent research in Roman London have appeared more sporadically in other periodicals including *Antiquity* (e.g., no. 64, 1990) and the *Archaeological Journal* (e.g., no. 148, 1991).

Southwark

There have been a series of interim reports in the *London Archaeologist* magazine, and a full colour booklet, *Recent Archaeological Excavations in Greater London*, edited by L. Blackmore *et al.*, (1990) which contain information on Roman development on the southern bank of the Thames.

More detailed reports on some of that work can be found in two major publications covering excavations from 1972 to 1974 and from 1973 to 1979, published jointly by LAMAS and the Surrey Archaeological Society (Special Papers nos 1 and 3). The later work is still being studied, and a series of important reports is being prepared for English Heritage by the MoLAS team, on the Winchester Palace site, for example.

Field records and archive reports

The original field records compiled on the City excavations 1973–91 are currently curated by the Museum of London; these records and the associated archive reports may be consulted by researchers who need access to them, but only by written request to the Archive Officer at the Museum.

Glossary

amphora (amphorae) Large pottery container used to transport commodities such as wine, olive oil or fish sauce; fragments of these vessels are a common find on London sites.

apse Semi-circular (or polygonal) chamber at the end of a hall; the second-century *basilica* and the third-century *mithraeum* were apsidal-ended buildings, for example.

basilica Aisled hall. The London basilica on the northern side of the forum served as the 'town hall', the administrative centre of Londinium.

Brickearth The orange-brown clay-like silt which caps the gravel terrace upon which Londinium was founded. It was extensively quarried to make bricks, hence its name.

colonia Class of town with a constitution based on that of Rome itself and which was governed by a charter. The inhabitants in the British *coloniae* (e.g., Colchester, Gloucester, Lincoln and York) included military veterans and their families: cf., *municipium*.

forum Heart of the civic centre. An open space used for meetings or markets, bounded in Londinium by ranges of offices or shops on three sides, with the great hall or basilica to the north.

insula Literally, 'island'. Describes block of land in a town bounded by streets on all sides.

legion/ *legio* In the first century AD, the Roman army was divided into some 30 legions, each with up to 6000 men. Four legions, supported by auxiliary troops, were required for the initial invasion of Britain: *II Augusta*, *IX Hispana*, *XIV Gemina* and *XX Valeria*. Other legions which served in the province (and which therefore might have sent detachments to Londinium) include *II Adiutrix* and *VI Victrix*.

mansio An inn or staging post, used by travellers and the imperial mail.

mithraeum A temple dedicated to the worship of Mithras, a wide spread religion which developed in Persia. It was a male-orientated cult, popular with soldiers and merchants.

municipium Class of town, governed by a charter and with a constitution based on Latin law. A *municipium* could be upgraded to the status of a *colonia*.

ordo Town council made up of some one hundred of the wealthier citizens.

tegula (tegulae) ceramic roof tile.

Place names

Blatobulgium Birrens
Burrium Usk
Calleva Silchester
Camulodunum Colchester
Clausentum Bitterne
Corinium Cirencester
Deva Chester
Dubris Dover

Durovernum Canterbury
Eburacum York
Glevum Gloucester
Isca Caerleon
Isca Dumnoniorum Exeter
Lemanis Lympne
Lindum Lincoln
Londinium London

Luguvalium Carlisle
Noviomagus Chichester
Ratae Leicester
Rutupiae Richborough
Venta Caistor-by-Norwich
Venonis High Cross
Verulamium St Albans
Viroconium Wroxeter

Index

(Page numbers in **bold** refer to illustrations)

Agricola, Julius 16
Albinus, Clodius 16
Aldersgate 78
Aldgate, **12**, 44, 46, 55, 78,
    excavations at 24, 28, 43, 87, 109
Aldwych 89
All Hallows by the Tower 121, **121**
Allectus, 38, 76, 96
    possible palace for, 76, **77**, 87, 93,
    colour plate 11
altars 65, 75, 113, 114, **114**, 115
America Square excavations 78
amphitheatre **12**, 26, 36, 53, 58, 59, **60**, **61**,
    87, 90, 121, **121**
amphora (amphorae) 30, 46, 52, 66, 69,
    117, 125
Anglo-Saxon Chronicle 18, 19
animal remains from London 50, 52, 73,
    106-10, **110**, 112
Antonine Itinerary 16, **17**
archive reports 25, 29, 90, 124
Arles (France), Council of 18
Arras medallion, 17
Arretium (Italy) 118
artefact studies 25–6, 29, 30, **30**, 32, 72, 73,
    106; see also amphorae, pottery, coins
Asia Minor 114
Athens (Greece) 118
Atrebates 41
Augusta 18, 19, 86, 87, **95**, 96
Austin Friars excavations 41, **74**, 75

Bank of England excavations 60, 61, **73**,
    110, 120, **121**
barrels 54, 117
basilica 26, 90, 94, 120, **121**, 124, 125; see
    also forum
    first phase c. AD 70+ 52, **52**, 53
    second phase c. AD 90+ 56, 57, **57**, 58,
    58, 59, **91**, **91**, **colour plate 9**
    demolition 81, 88
    reconstruction 98–101, **100**, **101**
Basinghall Street excavations 59
bastions 26, 85, **85**; see also wall, landward
bath-house 53, **54**, **59**, 59, **67**, 86, 121, **121**;
    see also Cheapside, Huggin Hill
Baynard's Castle excavations 32, 75, **76**,
    84, 84, 85, 113, 114

Bede, the Venerable 19, 88, 89
Biddle, M. 39, 88, 89
Billingsgate excavations 24, 46, 79, 86, 89,
    109, 121
Billiter Street excavations 44, 75
Birchin Lane excavations 26, 48, **colour
    plate 7**
bird remains from London 50, 106–8, **107**
Bishop of London 18–19
Bishopsgate **12**, 13, 18, 112
    excavations at 41, 43, 50, 75
Blackfriars ship 24, 38, 103-5, **104**, 122,
    124; see also ships
Blomfield House excavations 78, 85
bone-working 61, 109–10
botanical remains 41, 46, 49, 50, 64, 108
Boudica, rebellion of 16, 33, 39, 42, 44, 46,
    47, 48, 49, 50, 88, 93, 110, 114
Boulogne (France), 18
Bow Lane excavations 44, 55
Brickearth 37, 40, 49, 125
bridges 15, 26, 64, **64**, 65, 66, 84, 90
    reconstruction 101–3, **102**
Brigham, T. 91, 99, 101, 102
Britannia (journal) 124
Britannia (province) 32, 42, 94, **95**
    Inferior **95**,
    Superior 16, **95**
British Museum 20, 23, 115, 116, 117, 121
Brockley Hill 117
Bucklersbury excavations 23, **47**, 64, 66,
    75, 109
buildings, domestic **67**, **colour plates 1–3**;
    see also roundhouses
    brickearth-built 48, 49, **49**, **62**, 71, 72,
    74
    masonry-built 48, **54**, 55, 66, 68, **68**,
    69, 73, **74**, **75**, 86, 87, **86**, **87**, 89
    timber-built **47**, 48, 51, **51**, 53, 59, 61,
    62, 63, 71, 72, 78, 97, 98, **98**

Caesar, Julius 41
Calvert's Buildings SE1, excavations 115
Camulodunum (Colchester) 16, **17**, 19, 42,
    44, 47, 94, **95**
Cannon Street Station excavations 93, 98
Cantii 16, 41
Carausius 38

Catuvellauni 41
celtic language 41, 114
cemeteries 26, 43, **43**, 44, 48, 49, **49**, 85,
    87, **88**, 110-2, **111**, **112**; see also
    funerary monuments
Chapman, H. 24, 124
Cheapside,
    excavations 43, 45, 46, 48, 87
    bath-house 53, 59
City of London Archaeological Society
    (CoLAS) 24
Clare Street excavations 110
Classicianus, Julius, 114, 120
Classis Britannica 115–6
Clements Lane excavations 43
coins,
    for dating 32, 33, **33**, 84, 85, 87
    from London mint 116–7
    forgeries 34, 78, 124
    hoards 34, 65, 76, 78, 84, 85, 103
colonia 16, 39, 94
commerce 16, 30, 46, 66, 117–8; see also
    merchants
Constantius Chlorus 18
Copthall Avenue and Close excavations
    27, **28**, 61, **62**, 74, 97, 110, **colour
    plate 3**
Cornhill 40, 42, 44, 48, 94, 120
Corporation of London 11, 20, 22, 23, 24,
    26, 30, 31
Cottrill, F. 21
Council for British Archaeology 123
County Hall ship 38; see also ships
Courage Brewery site SE1 69, 97, 115
Covent Garden excavations 89
Crayford (*Creeganford*, Kent) 19
Crescent excavations 85
Cripplegate Fort 11, **12**, 58, 59, **59**, 63, 77,
    78, 93, 96, 115, 120, **121**
Crosswall excavations **77**, **85**, **118**, 119,
    120
cullet, see glass-working
Cullum Street excavations 43
curses 65, 114, 118, 119
Custom House excavations 24, 35, 37, 79
custom house in Londinium **64**, 65, 66

dark earth, problems of interpretation,

71–3, **colour plate 12**
Davies, B. 10, 35
defences, *see* Cripplegate Fort, bastions, wall
dendrochronology,
development in London 35–8
results 38, 43, 48, 53, 64, 65, 76, 78, 98
Department of the Environment (DoE) 11, 24, 30, 31; *see also* English Heritage
Department of Greater London Archaeology (DoGLA) 13, 25, 31, 89, 110
Department of Urban Archaeology (DUA) 10, 11, 12, 13, 24, 25, 26, 28, 31, 32, 39, 52, 71, 79, 88, 89, 90, 106
diatoma (microscopic algae) 39
Dio, Cassio 15
Docklands Light Railway excavations 15, 27, **47**
Domitian 94
Dover (Dubris) 16, **17**, 81, 115
Dowgate Hill House excavations 35, 62
drains, drainage 26, 59, 60, **60**, 66, **66**, 82, 108, 109, 110
Dunning, G. 21, **21**, 42, 91

Eastcheap excavations 48, 50
Eburacum (York) 16, **17**, **95**, 96
Eccles (Kent) 46
English Heritage 11, 12, 23, 31, 37, 124
environmental studies 40–1, 49–50, 52, 106–12, **106**; *see also* animal remains, bird remains, botanical remains, dendrochronology, diatoma, fish remains, human remains, river level change, soil micromorphology
Eumenius 17
excavation techniques 11, 20–8, **25**, **27**, **28**, **29**, **65**, **106**

farming, evidence of, 47, **49**, 50, 108–9
Fenchurch Street excavations 24, 43, 44, 45, 46, 48, **52**, 53, 69, **colour plate 8**
ferry 42, **43**, 54, **55**, **64**
Finsbury Circus excavations 41
fish remains from London 52, 107–8; *see also* fish sauce
fish sauce,
imported 30, 66, 69, 117
British 46, 108
Fish Street Hill excavations 46, **64**, 65, 66
Fishbourne (Sussex) 91
Fleet (river) 35, 40, **40**, 75, 78, 120
Fleet Street excavations 43
Fleet Valley excavations 64
Foster Lane excavations 72
fort 59; *see also* Cripplegate Fort
forum, 24, 27, 55, 94, 125; *see also* basilica
first phase *c.* AD 70+ 44, 52, **52**, 53, **57**,
second phase *c.* AD 90+ **12**, 56, 57, **57**, 58, 59, 101,
funerary monuments, 15, 85, 113, 114, 115, 118, **118**, 119; *see also* cemeteries

Gaul (France) 46, 66
Giltspur Street excavations 41, 111–12, **111**, **112**
glass
-working 46, 63, **63**, 74 *see also* tank furnace

vessels 66
Goodburn, D. 98, 104, **104**
Governor of province (Imperial legate) 16, 47, 58, 84, 91, 113, 114
'Governor's Palace' reinterpretation 91–3, **92**
Gracechurch Street, 51
excavations at, 27, 41, 44, 52, **53**, 120
graffiti 15, 113, 115, 117, 118, 119
Great St Helen's excavations 75
Greece 114, 117; *see also* Athens
Grew, F. 10, 123
Grimes, W.F. 10, 11, 21, 22, **22**, 59, 62, 71, 123, 124
Guildhall Museum 21, 23, 24, 25, 31, 59, 79, 86, 106
Guildhall Yard excavations 53, **60**, **61**, 63; *see also* amphitheatre
Gutter Lane excavations 68, 75

Hadrian 16, 88, 110
Hadrianic Fire 33, 72, 115
Hall, J. 10, 33, 123
Hebditch, M. 24
Hillam, J. 10, 37
hoofprints, of pack horses, 57, 107
Huggin Hill bath-house excavations 24, 30, 46, 53, **54**, 59, **59**, 74, 90, 93, 113, 117, 121, **121**
human remains, studies of, 110, 111–2, **111**, **112**; *see also* cemeteries
hypocaust, 59, 75, 82, **87**, 91

industrial activity 61, 63, 63, 69, 116, 117
ingots 117,
inscriptions 15, 70, 113-19, **114**, **116**, **118**
Institute of Archaeology 13; *see also* University College London
intaglios 46
Ironmonger Lane excavations 48, 55
iron-working 29, 61
Isis, temple of 113

Jewry Street excavations 85

Kent 19, 118
King, A. 109
King's Arms Yard 60
King Street excavations 82

Lea (river) 81
Leadenhall Court excavations **29**, 33, 35, 43, 48, **49**, 50, **51**, **52**, 56, 57, **58**, **83**, 107, 120, **121**, **colour plate 9**
Leadenhall Street excavations 80
leather-working 61, 62, 63, **63**, 109
legions 115, 125
Legio II Augusta 115
Legio VI Victrix 115
Legio XX Valeria Victrix 115
Lime Street excavations 48
Lindum (Lincoln) 18
Lombard Street excavations 44
Londinium, references to in classical sources, 16–19, 42, 114
London Archaeologist (journal) 124
London and Middlesex Archaeological Society 124
London Clay 39, 46
London Museum 21, 25

London Wall excavations 62, **62**, 110
Lorteburn (river) 40, **40**, 44
Lothbury excavations 75
Ludgate **12**, 40, 78
Ludgate Hill excavation 118
Luguvalio ad Vallum (Carlisle) 16, **17**
Lundenwic, mid-Saxon settlement, 89
Lupicinus 18

mansio 55, 82, 125
Marcellinus, Ammianus 18
Marsden, P. 10, 11, 24, 72, 91, 124
Marsh, G. 35
merchants in London, evidence of, 16, 30, 46, 66, 113, 117, 118
Mercury, statue of, 63 **colour plate 4**
Merrifield, R. 10, 24, 110, 123
Merriman, N. 41
Metunus (Neptune) 114, 118
middens 49, 108
Miles Lane excavations 54, 66, 107
military
artefacts, 43, 68, 115, 116
names of, 115–6, **116**
presence in London, 32, 39, 42, 43, 58, 59, 70, 112, 113, 114–6
Milk Street excavations 37, **70**, 82, **colour plate 12**
mills, millstones 46, 64,
mint 116–7
Mithraeum (temple of Mithras) 22, 23, 75, 113, 120, **121**, 124, 125
Mons Graupius (Scotland) 94
monumental arch 75, **76**
Moorgate, 78, 112
excavations, 63, **63**, 74, 110, **colour plate 4**
mosaic pavement 32, 68, 69, **70**, **73**, 75, 91, 120, 122, **colour plate 12**
municipium 19, 46, 94, 125; *see also* colonia
Museum of London (MoL) 10, 12, 25, 26, 38, 101, 104, 105, 113, **121**, 122, 124
Museum of London Archaeology Service (MoLAS) 10, 31

names of persons who lived in Londinium
children 114, 118
men 114–8; *see also* military
women 119
National Safe Deposit Bank excavations 64
neonates 50; *see also* animal remains
Newgate **12**, 44, 46, **67**, 78
Newgate Street excavations 35, **44**, 45, **45**, **67**, 68, **71**, 72, 90, **colour plates 1** and 2
Noble Street excavations 11
Noel-Hume, I. **23**, 24
Notitia Dignitatum 18
Noviomagus (Rochester) 16, **17**

Old Bailey excavations 24, 75, 78, 82
Old Broad Street excavations 64
Old Ford E8 81
olive oil 30, 46, 66
opus signinum (op. sig.) floor **29**, 69, 91, 99
opus spicatum floor 99
Ordnance Datum (OD) 39
ordo 88, 125
Oswald, A. 24

oysters 108

Pepys Street, aisled hall at, 87
Perring, D. 10, 47, 123
Philp, B. 24
Pinner Hall excavations 64
plague 73
Planning Policy Guidance Note 16 (PPG16) 30
Portus Lemanis (Lympne) 16, **17**
post-excavation techniques 29, **35**
pottery 113
    made in London, 34, 46, 61
    imported, 34, **36**, 46, **colour plate 10**
    used for dating, 32, 34, **34**, 35, **35**, 44, 46, 72, 73, 87; *see also* Roman Ceramic Phases
prehistoric finds from London 41
Procurator 114, 119
Provincial Council 113, 118, 119
Ptolemeus, Claudius, 16
public building programmes 55–8, 68–70, 75, 77, 79; *see also* basilica, bath-house, forum, quays, wall
Pudding Lane excavations **25**, 38, 42, **64**, **65**, **66**, **67**, 86, **86**, **87**, 89, 97, **colour plate 6**

quarries 26, 43, 44, 46
quays **21**, **25**, 26, 27, **37**, 38, 49, 53, 54, **64**, 65, **66**, **66**, 68, 78, 79, **80**, 81, **82**, 89, 94, 102, 103, 105, 121, 122
Queen Street excavations 51, **51**

radiocarbon dating 32
Ravenna Cosmography 19
Reculver 81
Regis House excavations 21, 54, 66, 108
Regno (Chichester) 16, **17**
religious practices 106, 110; *see also* altars, cemeteries, funerary monuments, temples, votive offerings
rivers; *see* Fleet, Lea, Lorteburn, Thames, Walbrook
river/sea-level change 39, 79, **80**, 81, 96
Roach Smith, C. 20, 30, 65, 106, 122
roads
    in Roman London, 26, 27, 39, **41**, **43**, 44, 46, 47, 51, **55**, 56, 59, **59**, 61, 66, 69, 82, **83**, 87, 88, 101
    leading to or from London 16, **17**, 39, 42, 43, 81
Roman and Medieval London Excavation Council (RMLEC) 21, 22, **22**, 23, 25, 28, 31, 106
Roman Ceramic Phases 35
round-houses 44, 45
Royal Commission on Historical Monuments (RCHM) 15

Rutupiae (Richborough) 16, **17**, 18, 42, 81, 115

St Bartholomew's Hospital excavations 112
St Bride's Church excavations 23, 43, 87, 121, **121**
St Magnus House excavations 35, 37, 89
St Martin le Grand 44
St Martin Ludgate excavations 78
St Martin Orgar excavations 41
St Mary Aldermanbury 23
St Mary at Hill 41
St Mary Axe excavations 85
St Paul's Cathedral 40, 44
St Peter's Hill excavations 38, 75, 76, **77**, 87, 93, **colour plate 11**
St Swithin's House excavations **23**, 62, 110
St Swithin's Lane excavations 48
Seal House excavations 37
Seething Lane excavations 41
Septimius Severus 78
Shadwell signal station E 85
Sheffield University 37
Sheldon, H. 72
ships in Londinium 78, 105, 116, 117; *see also* Blackfriars, County Hall
Silures 16
slaves 114, 118, 119
Society of Antiquaries of London 20, 21, 31
soil micromorphology 50, 72
Southwark SE1, 25, 39, 40, **40**, 41, 43, 48, 103, 109, 113, 114, 115, 119, 124
    Roman developments in **41**, 48, 55, 69, 72, 73, 82, 84, 90, 97
stamps 114
stamped tiles 114, 115, 116, 117
status of Londinium 88, 94–6; *see also colonia, municipium*
Suetonius 16
Sugar Loaf Court ware 34, 46
Swan Lane excavations 68, 79

Tacitus, Cornelius, 16, 19, 39, 46
temples **52**, 53, 65, 75, 82, 114; *see also* Isis, Mithraeum
tessellated pavement 69, **69**, 75, 120, 121
Thames (river) **12**, 15, 19, 39, 40, **40**, 41, **41**, 42, 43, 46, 53, 64, 78, 79, **80**, 107, 111, 114
    crossing 40, 42, 46, 52, 54, 101, 103; *see also* bridges)
Thames Exchange excavations **37**, **82**
Thames Street excavations 27, 37
Theodosius 18
Thorney Island 42
Threadneedle Street excavations 27

Tower Hill Pageant 103, 105, **121**, 122
Tower of London excavations 41, 78, 84, 85, 112
Treasury at London 18, 19
Trinovantes 41
Tyers, I. 10, 30, 38
Tyers, P. 10, 35

University College London 10, 13; (*see also* Institute of Archaeology)

Verulamium (St Albans) 16, 19, 34, 47, 81
Venta Caistor 16, **17**
Vindolanda (on Hadrian's Wall) 115
Vintry excavations 78, 79
votive offerings 65, 84, 110, 111, 116

Walbrook (river) 40, **40**, 84, **92**, 93
    development of valley, 44, 46, 54, 56, 60–4, **62**, **63**, 66, 73, 74, 93, 97, 110, 120, 123, 124
    finds from 35, 61–4, 66, 110, 115, 117, 118, 120, 124
Waldron, T. 10, 110
wall, defending Londinium, **12**, **88**, 120, **121**; *see also* bastions
    landward 77, **77**, 78, 85, **85**, 88, 94
    riverside 26, 38, **76**, 84, 88, 90, 124
wall plaster 49, 51, 52, 53, **68**, 69, 75, 122, **colour plate 8**
warehouses 26, 54, 64, 64, 65, **65**, 66, **66**, 86
Warwick Square excavations 44
waterfront development, 46, 53–4, 66, 68, 78–81, **80**, 87, 89 **colour plate 5**; *see also* bridges, quays, warehouses, watermills, *see* mills
water-pipes 75, 110
Watling Court excavations 37, 48, 68
Well Court excavations 46, 48
wells 26, 50, 106, 108
West, B. 10, 72
West Tenter Street excavations 107, 111
Westminster 42, 114
Wheeler, Sir M. 88
Whittington Avenue excavations 43, 44, 48, 50, **69**
Winchester Palace site SE1 69, 70, 84, 93, 113, 115
wine
    British 117
    imported 66, 69
workshops 61, 63, **63**, 64
writing tablets 15, 113, 117, 118

York (Eburacum) 18, 96
Yule, B. 72